# EXPLORING THE WORLD

## S T U D E N T   W O R K B O O K

to accompany EXPLORING THE WORLD, 3rd Edition

## Nona Starr, CTC

TheTravel institute

# Contents

# Introduction

The Workbook has practice worksheets and resource materials such as Web sites and a selected list of World Heritage Sites for your use in research and reinforcement. Once you start exploring travel sites on the Internet—and be warned, there are literally millions—you will be able to plan a trip from A to Z.

Newspapers, periodicals, guidebooks, and books about the travel experience fill the need for background information, but you will rarely find such items in the offices of the travel, tourism, and hospitality industry. Almost every resource is online. The time needed to produce and print hard copy has made the Internet the resource of choice. The telephone has given way to e-mail and fax communication.

Fiction can enhance a travel experience—especially when the reader wants to wile away time during travel or settle the mind before bedtime. Each chapter in this Workbook has reading suggestions, some of historical and educational interest, some just for fun.

## ■ Travel on the Internet

Typically, an Internet site is an extension of an established business, be it an airline, hotel chain, railroad, cruise line, ground transportation provider, tour operator, travel agency, convention and visitors' bureau (CVB), or destination's marketing office. Some are Web-only travel agencies—such as Expedia or Travelocity—designed to serve travelers who want to book trips themselves. Others are owned by groups of airlines or hotels. Still others are set up by local or foreign tourist bureaus and businesses to sell their regions and products. Always consider the source. Most well-known names in travel are on the Web. But anyone can put up a site. If the name is not familiar, check further. Be aware that the Web is constantly changing. Sites merge, change, or go out of business without warning. The goals of this Workbook are to help you recognize useful sites and start building your own electronic address book. Inclusion in this book does not represent endorsement by The Travel Institute.

Note that when Internet identifying codes are used at the end of a Web site, they let a user know where the site is located. For example, in Chapter 15—The Pacific—when you see www.railaustralia.com.au, you might notice that the Web site ends with au, the country code for Australia. It means that the site is actually located in Australia. Other Web international addresses end in such suffixes as eu and asia.

Each Workbook chapter lists Web sites in its Resources section. Just about every travel and tourism organization seems to have one. You can usually find what you want by simply putting in the name or term of what you are looking for and letting your search engine do the work. The way to become an expert is to dig in and practice. Sometimes the best way to learn the Web is simply to keep traveling on it.

# ■ Attractions

As well as commercial attractions such as Walt Disney World, a country's national parks, battlefields, memorials, historic sites, monuments, preserves, seashores, parkways, lakeshores, wild and scenic rivers, trails, and recreation areas attract travelers and spin off business, especially to the industry's tourism and hospitality segments. In the United States, national park sites are authorized for protection by Congress or by presidential proclamation. Today, more than 84 million acres of federal land are administered by the National Park Service (NPS). Those initials appear in a park's Web address.

Private organizations, such as National Trusts, also contribute to the preservation of a country's heritage. Some organizations are privately funded, such as the British Isles National Trusts; others have limited government protection.

In the United States, the Travel Industry Association (TIA), in cooperation with the NPS, has a marketing campaign designed to raise awareness and encourage visits to national parks. Its Web site (www.seeamerica.org) has information on national parks and tours.

# ■ UNESCO

The United Nations Educational, Scientific, and Cultural Organization (UNESCO) is an autonomous agency of the United Nations (UN). It has developed the World Heritage List, a list of places of importance to tourism because of either their natural heritage or their significant contribution to world culture. Some sites are both natural and cultural.

To be on the list, countries that are signatories to the World Heritage Convention submit potential sites to UNESCO, which then considers each proposal. Sites listed with an asterisk (*) are places of "World Heritage in Danger."

You might notice that the United States has few places on either the cultural or natural list. The United States boycotted UNESCO for 19 years, finally rejoining in 2003. During the boycott, the United States did not submit any sites for consideration.

Most of the world's natural heritage sites are listed in this workbook, but due to space limitations, only a selected list of cultural heritage sites are. Sites are also added or deleted by UNESCO. Its Web site, www.unesco.org/whc, displays the most up-to-date list.

The cultural sites are one of the following types:
■ Places of historical interest.
■ Significant architectural works.
■ Monumental works of sculpture and painting.

- Archaeological sites.

   The natural sites are judged for the importance of the following characteristics:

- Significant natural features.
- Habitats of threatened species of outstanding value.
- Outstanding scientific or conservation value or natural beauty.

# CHAPTER 1

# Destination Geography

## ■ Resources

Travel companies are always seeking more efficient ways of doing business, particularly relating to technology. Increasing online presence is due in large part to the necessity to be in front of consumers, wherever and whenever they want information that might lead to a product sale.

### Accommodations

Industry references such as the *Hotel & Travel Index* and the *Star Service* are online with access by subscription. Most hotels, motels, and resorts have Web sites. They can be accessed by putting in the name of the hotel or its brand affiliation. Some sites list rates and specials; others have pictures and booking information. Although not a reference source for booking accommodations, the American Hotel & Motel Association is the trade association that represents the interests of the lodging industry. It provides information and support to its membership throughout the world.

American Hotel & Motel Association
www.ahma.com

### Air Travel

As well as being in the trade's Global Distribution Systems (GDSs), airlines host Web sites available to the consumer. Sites with background information that you might like to visit are:

Airlines Reporting Corporation (ARC)
www.arccorp.com

Guide to airports and 3-letter codes
www.quickaid.com

International Air Transport Association (IATA)
www.iatan.org

U.S. Department of Transportation
airconsumer.ost.dot.gov/

# Cruises

The cruise product continues to grow despite the world's economic and political problems. The product's flexibility is one of its big business advantages. Companies can move their products (ships) to avoid geopolitical hot spots and reroute them to calmer seas, perhaps to ports in Alaska, the Caribbean, or South America. There also has been an increase in "home-porting," which means ships originating from local ports instead of sailings from one port only. This attracts passengers who prefer to drive to the embarkation point instead of having to fly. Some thirty U.S. cities now operate as cruise ship gateways, roughly double the number in 2000.

Sixty percent of all cruise companies are under the umbrella of industry giant Carnival Corporation. The company fully or partially owns Carnival Cruise Lines, Costa Cruise Lines, Cunard Line, Holland America Line, Princess Cruises, Seabourn, and Windstar. Royal Caribbean International is another major player. It owns Royal Caribbean and Celebrity Cruises. For an overall view, visit www.cruising.org, the site for Cruise Line International (CLIA), the cruise industry's trade association.

Cruise line Web sites are listed in the Chapter 6 (Bermuda and the West Indies) resources box. Companies that specialize in one or two destinations only, such as river cruisers, are listed in appropriate chapters.

# Currency Questions and Travel Insurance

Information about travel insurance, tipping, and currency conversion is available from:

Currency exchange
www.xe.com

Travel insurance
www.accessamerica.com
www.travel-guard.com

# Destination Information

Web sites with destination information are:

Amusement parks
www.ticketforfun.com

*Condé Nast Traveler*
www.cntraveler.com

Fodor's Guides
www.fodors.com

Frommer's Guides
www.frommers.com

Lonely Planet Guides
www.lonelyplanet.com

Michelin Guides
www.michelin-travel.com

Moon Travel Handbooks
www.moon.com

*National Geographic*
www.nationalgeographic.com

National Geographic Traveler
www.nationalgeographic.com/traveler

Special interest travel
www.specialtytravel.com

Travel and Leisure
www.travelandleisure.com

World Travel Guide
www.wtgonline.com

Zagat Guides
www.zagat.com

Destination information is also available from trade associations that represent their member countries. They are:

African Travel Association
www.africa-ata.org

Caribbean Tourism Association
www.doitcaribbean.com

European Travel Commission
www.visiteurope.com

Pacific Asia Travel Association (PATA)
www.pata.org

# Events

Travelers often want to link their trips to a special event. For listings, you might try:

Arts, music, sports, and children's interests
www.festivals.com

Events listed by date, location, type
www.eventsworldwide.com

Guide to North American fairs
www.fairsnet.org

North American events
www.festivalfinder.com

# Government Resources

When questions involve safety, health, or customs and documentation regulations, travelers need reliable answers. U.S. government sources for information on health and safety are:

Centers for Disease Control (CDC)
www.cdc.gov/travel

Duty-free allowances
www.customs.ustreas.gov

Federal Aviation Administration
www.faa.gov

U.S. National Parks (alphabetical lists of parks with links to each park and photos)
www.nps.gov

U.S. Passport Office
www.uspassportinformation.gov

World Health Organization (a U.N. agency)
www.who.ch

At www.travel.state.gov/travel_warnings, the State Department provides:

1. **Consular information sheets** for each foreign country, with information about health, crime, and safety considerations. Consular information sheets are strictly factual and contain no advice on whether a traveler should or should not visit a country.

2. **Public announcements** issued when temporary conditions in a country create a security risk that might make someone think twice about going. Examples are terrorist threats, political demonstrations, anniversary dates of bombings, and events such as earthquakes. Public announcements have expiration dates and often are confined to a particular part of a country.

3. **Travel warnings**, the strongest type of release, are issued when the State Department recommends avoiding a country.

# Maps

The National Geographic Society (nationalgeographic.com) and publisher Rand McNally (www.randmcnally.com) provide maps online. Other handy sites include mapquest.com, freetrip.com, and mapsonus.com

Remember to credit the source if you print out a map (or get permission in writing if you intend to duplicate a map in any sales literature). Reproducing a map for anything but personal or educational purposes violates copyright laws.

# Road Travel

Web sites make it easy to compare rates and reserve a rental car anywhere in the world. You might want to begin your search with one of the online travel agencies. After you have found the best rate, check the car rental company's own site to see if there are any specials or other savings.

# Sports

For information about when and where events are scheduled or where to go to participate in a favorite sport, contact:

Baseball—major leagues
www.mlb.com

Basketball—National Basketball Association
www.nba.com

Bicycle tours
www.backroads.com

Diving—Association of Diving Instructors (PADI)
www.padi.com

Golf—United States Golf Association (USGA)
www.usga.org

Hiking—American Hiking Society
www.americanhiking.org

Ice hockey—National Hockey League
www.nhl.com

Nature—the Sierra Club
www.sierraclub.org/outings

Ski resorts
www.inter-ski.com

Tennis—U.S. Tennis Association
www.usta.com

# Time

Do time zone changes confuse you? The Internet provides help so that vacationers do not call home at 0200 or when everyone but the cat has gone to work. Try:

Local time provider
www.worldtimeserver.com

Time zone converter
www.timezoneconverter.com

# Tours

Regional and national tour operators are plentiful on the Web. Local tour operators are American Sightseeing International and Grayline Tours. The United States Tour Operators Association (USTOA) and NTA are trade associations representing international and domestic tour operators:

American Sightseeing International
www.sightseeing.com

Grayline Tours
www.grayline.com

United States Tour Operators Association (USTOA)
www.ustoa.com

# Weather

You can get 3- to 5-day forecasts for almost any place on earth from:

CNN weather forecasts
www.cnn.com/weather

Forecasts
www.accuweather.com

Hurricane tracking
www.fema.gov

National Weather Service
www.nws.noaa.gov

The Weather Channel
www.weather.com

## Using Information

After you have found information, you must judge its usefulness. Factors to consider are:

- **Date.** If you are doing research in rapidly changing areas such as price, schedule, or availability, you need an electronic resource. Be sure to check a site's posting date; some remain unchanged for a long time.

- **Authoritativeness.** Is the information correct? It may be wise to check facts with a second source.

- **Bias.** Does the information have any apparent bias? It would be a rare travel supplier, publication, tour operator, tourist board, hotel, convention and visitors' center, or restaurant site that mentions anything negative.

# Worksheet 1.1: Geography

_____

Name                                                                  Date

**Directions:** Answer the questions in the space provided. Answers can be found in your textbook or on a map.

1. What does the word _geography_ mean to you? How do you think knowledge of destination geography will benefit you as a travel professional?

   _____

   _____

2. How do cartographers shape our world?

   _____

   _____

3. What do geographers need to know about places on the earth?

   _____

   _____

4. Are lines of longitude and latitude all the same length?

   _____

5. What is a hemisphere? Which one do you live in?

   _____

   _____

6. How does a GPS unit know where you are?

   _____

   _____

7. What does the map's scale tell you?

   _____

8. Why are varying colors on a map sometimes used?

   _____

   _____

9. Which is the largest continent?

   _____

10. What legal implications does the location of a country's continental shelf have for the cruise industry?

_____

_____

11. What is an archipelago? Name three.

_____

_____

12. What is a strait? Name three.

_____

_____

13. Which is the world's largest country?

_____

14. Which country has the longest coastline?

_____

15. How does elevation affect climate?

_____

16. What is the jet stream? How does it affect an airplane's flight?

_____

17. How do you convert Fahrenheit to Celsius?

_____

18. What is a rain forest? Where are most located?

_____

19. What is a desert? Name three.

_____

_____

20. Name two barriers to travel that create cultural misunderstandings. Why do they do so?

_____

_____

# Worksheet 1.2: Answering Questions

_____

Name                                                                    Date

**Directions:** Answer each question in the space provided.

1. You are working at an airline reservations desk. The traveler asks, "How long is my flight from New York City to Los Angeles? From Los Angeles back to New York City? Why is there a difference?" How would you answer?

2. You are working for a bookstore that specializes in travel books. The customer asks, "What guidebook would you recommend for my trip to England? Why do you suggest that one?" How would you answer?

# Worksheet 1.3: Using Reference Materials

_____

Name                                                                  Date

**Directions:** Using available resources, answer the questions in the space provided. Indicate in your answer what resource you used.

1. What reference source would you consult to determine the health hazards of a trip to the Brazilian rain forest? Did the resource suggest any precautions? If so, what?

2. You need to know the documentation requirements for travel to Australia. Where would you look? What did you find out?

3. What will the weather be like for a cruise around the Horn of South America in March?

4. Ms. Te Kauri wants to know if her health insurance will cover her when she goes bungee-jumping on her New Zealand vacation. What do you tell her?

# Worksheet 1.4: Map Review

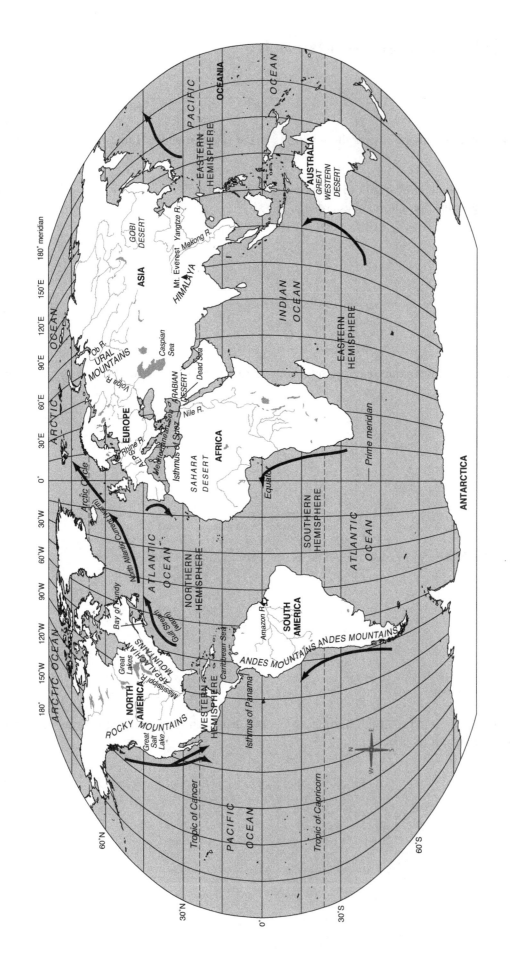

## FIGURE 1.1 Earth

▲ National park or other site
1 inch = 2,316 miles (3,726 km)

# Worksheet 1.4: Map Review

Name _____      Date _____

**Directions:** Using the map on the preceding page, answer the following questions.

1. What is the map's scale?

   _____

2. What feature on the map indicates its directional orientation?

   _____

3. Most people are familiar with the equator, but where would you be if you were at a latitude of 23.5° north of the equator, the farthest point at which the sun can be seen directly overhead at noon?

   _____

4. If you were to fly due west from Ireland to North America, you would reach the lower region of Hudson Bay in Canada, which is on the same latitude as Ireland. Why, then, is Ireland's climate so mild?

   _____

   _____

5. Name the mountain range that serves as a boundary between Europe and northern Asia.

   _____

6. The Appalachian Mountain Range is the principal mountain landform on North America's East Coast. Which mountain range is the West Coast's principal landform?

   _____

7. Which continent is the only one with land in all four hemispheres?

   _____

8. Which is the only continent other than Antarctica that does not extend into the tropics?

   _____

9. How many degrees of longitude would you cross to travel halfway around the world?

   _____

10. The equator is to latitude as which of the following is to longitude?
    A. Tropic of Cancer
    B. Tropic of Capricorn
    C. International date line
    D. Prime meridian

# Worksheet 1.5: Looking Back: A Chapter Quiz

Name _____     Date _____

**Directions:** Answer the questions in the space provided.

1. What is the shortest, most direct route between any two points on the surface of the earth?

   _____

2. Convert the following times from AM and PM to the 24-hour clock.

   A. 1:20 PM _____     C. 10:30 AM _____

   B. 8:08 AM _____     D. 11:59 PM _____

3. Convert the following times from the 24-hour clock to AM and PM.

   A. 1306 _____     C. 0800 _____

   B. 1845 _____     D. 2347 _____

4. Your usual method of international communication, the fax machine, is not working, and you need to contact a hotel in Vienna, Austria (GMT + 2). What time should you make a phone call to be assured that the hotel's reservations office will receive your call about 10:00 AM Vienna time?

   _____

5. If it rains on your golf game in Hawaii, is the cause climate or weather?

   _____

6. Why would a destination near the equator require a visitor to bring a heavy sweater?

   _____

   _____

7. Match each term with the correct definition. Write the definition's letter in the blank at the left of each term.

   _____ tropics          A. Cold or warm rivers of sea water.

   _____ rain shadow      B. Latitudes between the Tropic of Cancer and the Tropic of
                                         Capricorn.

   _____ trade winds      C. The dry area on the leeward side of a mountain.

   _____ westerlies       D. Constant winds that blow from the northeast toward the equator in
                                         the Northern Hemisphere and from the southeast toward the equator
                                         in the Southern Hemisphere.

   _____ ocean currents   E. Currents of air high above the earth, blowing from the southwest in
                                         the Northern Hemisphere and from the northwest in the Southern
                                         Hemisphere.

# CHAPTER 2

# The Eastern United States

## ■ Resources

In today's world, the Internet provides just about anything anyone wants to know. The ease of updating makes the Net's logistical information far more current than any paper resource. Even magazines are online. For trips to the southern states, the regional magazine *Southern Living* (www.southernliving. com) offers destination news, and *Yankee Magazine* (www.yankeemagazine. com) aids travelers to New England. *Midwest Living* and *Sunset* are sources for their regions. See their Web listings in Chapters 3 and 4.

American Cruise Lines
www.americancruiselines.com

U.S. rail travel
www.amtrak.com

### Alabama
www.touralabama.org

Mobile
www.mobile.org

### Connecticut
www.tourism.state.ct

Foxwoods
www.foxwoods.com

Mystic Seaport
www.visitmystic.com

### Delaware
www.state.de.us/tourism

Brandywine Valley
www.visitwilmingtonde.com

### District of Columbia
www.washington.org

Ford's Theatre
www.fordstheatre.org

Kennedy Center
www.kennedy-center.org

Mount Vernon
www.mountvernon.org

Smithsonian Museums
www.si.edu

White House
www.nps.gov/whho

## Florida
www.flausa.com

Amelia Island
www.ameliaisland.com

Everglades
www.nps.gov/ever

Florida Keys
www.fla-keys.com

Fort Lauderdale
www.sunny.org

Fort Myers/Sanibel
www.leeislandcoast.com

Kennedy Space Center
www.kennedyspacecenter.com

Marco Island
www.marcoislandchamber.org

Miami
www.miamiandbeaches.com

Orlando
www.orlandoinfo.com

Palm Beach
www.palmbeachfl.com

Pensacola
www.relaxinpensacola.com

Sea World/Busch Gardens
www.4adventure.com

Universal Studios Florida
www.universalstudios.com

Villa Vizcaya
www.vizcayamuseum.com

Walt Disney World
www.disneyworld.com

## Georgia
www.georgiatourism.com

Atlanta
www.atlanta.com

Golden Isles
www.bgicvb.com

Savannah
www.savannahvisit.com

## Kentucky
www.kentuckytourism.com

Lexington
www.visitlex.com

## Louisiana
www.louisianatravel.com

Lafayette
www.lafayettetravel.com

New Orleans
www.neworleanscvb.com

## Maine
www.visitmaine.com

Acadia National Park
www.nps.gov/acad

Kennebunk
www.visitthekennebunks.com

Sunday River
www.sundayriver.com

Windjammers
www.mainewindjammers.com

## Maryland
www.maryland.com

Annapolis
www.visit-annapolis.org

Baltimore
www.baltimore.org

Chesapeake Bay cruises
www.chesapeakebaycruises.com

## Massachusetts
www.massvacation.com

Berkshires
www.berkshires.org

Boston
www.bostonusa.com

Boston North
www.northofboston.org

Cape Cod
www.capecodchamber.org

Freedom Trail
www.thefreedomtrail.org

Martha's Vineyard
www.mvy.com

## Mississippi
www.visitmississippi.org

Biloxi-Gulfport
www.gulfcoast.org

Natchez
www.natchez.ms

Natchez Trace
www.scenictrace.com

Tupelo
www.tupelo.net

Vicksburg
www.visitvicksburg.com

## New Hampshire
www.visitnh.com

Attitash
www.attitash.com

Bretton Woods
www.brettonwoods.com

Cog Railway
www.thecog.com

Waterville Valley
www.waterville.com

## New Jersey
www.newjerseychamber.com

Atlantic City
www.atlanticcitynj.com

Cape May
www.capemaychamber.com

## New York
www.iloveny.state.ny

Catskill Region
www.catskills.com

Empire State Building
www.esbnyc.com

Finger Lakes
www.fingerlakes.org

Long Island
www.licvb.com

New York City
www.nycvisit.com

Niagara Falls
www.niagarafalls.com

Playbill (NYC theaters)
www.playbill.com

Statue of Liberty
www.nps.gov/stli

Theater tickets
www.theatredirect.com

Thousand Islands
www.visit1000islands.com

## North Carolina
www.visitnc.com

Asheville
www.exploreasheville.org

Biltmore Estate
www.biltmore.com

Outer Banks
www.outerbanks.org

## Pennsylvania

www.visitpa.com

Bucks County
www.experiencebuckscounty.com

Gettysburg
www.gettyburgcvb.org

Lancaster County
www.padutchcountry.com

National Constitution Center
www.constitutioncenter.org

Philadelphia
www.gophila.org

Pittsburgh
www.pittsburgh.com

Valley Forge
www.valleyforge.org

## Rhode Island

www.visitrhodeisland.com

Block Island
www.blockislandchamber.com

Newport
www.gonewport.com

Newport mansions
www.newportmansions.org

Providence
www.goprovidence.com

## South Carolina

www.travelsc.com

Charleston
www.charlestoncvb.com

Hilton Head
www.hiltonheadisland.org

Low Country
www.southcarolinalowcountry.com

Myrtle Beach
www.myrtlebeach.org

Sea Pines
www.seapines.com

## Tennessee

www.state.tn.us

Chattanooga
www.chattanoogafun.com

Dollywood
www.dollywood.com

Graceland
www.elvis.com

Grand Ole Opry
www.opry.com

Memphis
www.memphistravel.com

Nashville
www.nashvillecvb.com

## Vermont

www.travelvermont.com

Killington
www.killington.com

Lake Champlain CVB
www.vermont.org

Mount Snow
www.mountsnow.com

Smugglers' Notch
www.smuggs.com

Stowe
www.stowe.com

Stratton Mountain
www.strattton.com

Sugarbush
www.sugarbush.com

## Virginia

www.virginia.org

Blue Ridge Parkway
www.nps.gov/blri

Northern Virginia
www.visitnorthernvirginia.com

Virginia Beach
www.vbfun.com

Williamsburg
www.colonialwilliamsburg.com

Wolf Trap Park
www.wolftrap.org

**West Virginia**

www.westvirginia.com

Charleston
www.charlestonwv.com

state parks
www.wvstateparks.com

# ■ UNESCO World Heritage Sites

For the Eastern United States, the UNESCO World Heritage List includes the following:

## Cultural Heritage

- Independence Hall, Pennsylvania

- Monticello and the University of Virginia, Virginia

- Statue of Liberty, New York

## Natural Heritage

- *Everglades National Park, Florida

- Great Smoky Mountains National Park, Tennessee and North Carolina

- Mammoth Cave National Park, Kentucky

# ■ Reading Suggestions: The Eastern United States

- Louisa May Alcott (1832–1888): Her novels *Little Women* and *Little Men*, written to contribute to the family income, have become classics; her childhood home in Concord, Massachusetts, is a tourist attraction.

- John Berendt: *Midnight in the Garden of Good and Evil* (1994) covers society life and murder in Savannah, Georgia.

- Bruce Catton: *A Stillness at Appomattox* (1953) is the Pulitzer Prize–winning final volume of his *Army of the Potomac* trilogy.

- Frank Conroy: *Time and Tides: A Walk through Nantucket* (2004) is a story about the island's evolution from an isolated whalers' station to one of the most prestigious vacation addresses on the East Coast.

- John Jakes: *North and South* (1982) is a Civil War potboiler.

- Frances Parkinson Keys: *Dinner at Antoine's* (1948) is a murder mystery set in New Orleans a few weeks before Mardi Gras.

- Henry Wadsworth Longfellow (1807–1882): His narrative poems *Evangeline*, *Hiawatha*, *The Courtship of Miles Standish*, *Paul Revere's Ride*, and *Tales of a Wayside Inn* did a great deal to develop audiences for poetry in America.

- James Michener: *Chesapeake* (1978) is a history of the bay.

- Margaret Mitchell: *Gone with the Wind* (1936) is a Civil War novel and the winner of a Pulitzer Prize, with more than 20 million copies in 27 languages.

- Michael Sharra: *The Killer Angels* (1975) is the Civil War's Battle of Gettysburg. Work of Jeff Sharra continues his father's epics.

- Les Standiford: *Last Train to Paradise* (2002) is the story of Henry Flagler's dream to build a railroad across the sea to Key West.

- Smithsonian series: *The Smithsonian Guides to Historic America* (many revisions) is an easy-to-read series with many pictures, good reference material.

# Worksheet 2.1: Geography

Name _____ Date _____

**Directions:** Answer the questions in the space provided. Answers can be found by looking either in your textbook or at a map.

1. Name three barrier islands off the East Coast of the United States.

   _____

   _____

2. What does it mean when geographers say a place is part of an area called the Piedmont? Give an example of a state where the Piedmont is most obvious.

   _____

   _____

3. Why did the fall line limit explorers' ship travel?

   _____

   _____

4. What mountain system stretches north–south from Canada to Alabama? Name at least three of its ranges.

   _____

   _____

5. What is a delta?

   _____

   _____

6. Why was the Erie Canal so important in its time?

   _____

   _____

7. How has New York City's solid rock base helped the city to grow?

   _____

   _____

8. How does the word *capital* differ in meaning from the word *capitol*?

_____

_____

9. Why are graves aboveground in Louisiana?

_____

_____

10. How would you describe the landscape around Walt Disney World in Florida?

_____

_____

# Worksheet 2.2: Itinerary Planning

_____
Name                                                                     Date

The travelers, a couple in their twenties, are spending a long weekend (3 days) in New Orleans. You are working for the city's tourist board, and they come to you for information about what to see and do in the city. What questions do you ask the couple before you make recommendations? It is not enough to ask where they have been in the past or what hotels they have used. Good customer relationship management must include gathering as much knowledge as possible about what makes potential customers tick. Outline their answers before you make suggestions.

# Worksheet 2.3: Answering Questions

_____
Name                                                                      Date

**Directions:** How would you respond to travelers who ask the following questions?

1. "Aren't New York City theater tickets too expensive?"

2. "You recommend using public transportation in the big cities. Aren't subway systems dangerous?"

3. A traveler who lives in Maryland says: "My daughter, who lives in central Florida, and I would like to meet midway in late March. Do you have any suggestions for a destination where we could shop, relax, and do a little sightseeing? Neither of us plays golf, and I no longer enjoy sitting on the beach for hours."

4. "What do you do at a theme park if it rains or gets hot?"

# Worksheet 2.4: Map Review

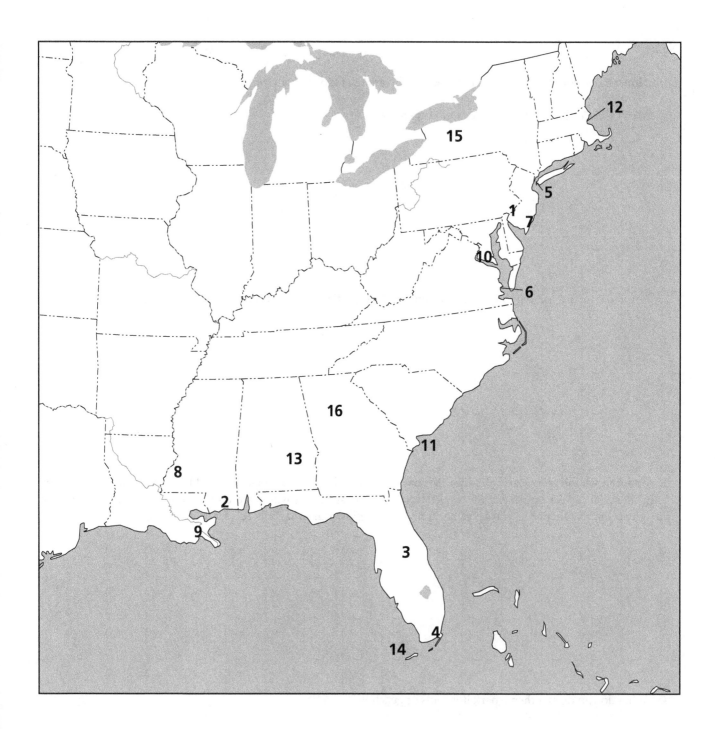

# Worksheet 2.4: Map Review

_____

Name                                                                    Date

**Directions:** In the following exercises, give the three-letter airport code of the destination or of the nearest airport city. Use industry or Internet resources to find the codes.

1. Match the New England or New York destination with its number on the map.

   **Map Number**                              **Airport Code**

   _____        Broadway            _____

   _____        Finger Lakes        _____

   _____        Faneuil Hall        _____

2. Match the Mid-Atlantic destination with its number on the map.

   _____        Atlantic City       _____

   _____        Liberty Bell        _____

   _____        Mount Vernon        _____

3. Match the southern destination with its number on the map.

   _____        Atlanta             _____

   _____        Hilton Head         _____

   _____        Williamsburg        _____

4. Match the Florida destination with its number on the map.

   _____        Key West            _____

   _____        South Beach         _____

   _____        Walt Disney World   _____

5. Match the Gulf Coast destination with its number on the map.

   _____        Bourbon Street           _____

   _____        Gulfport                 _____

   _____        Memorial Baptist Church  _____

   _____        Natchez                  _____

# Worksheet 2.5: Using Reference Materials

Name                                                                Date

**Directions:** Using available resources, answer the questions in the space provided. Indicate in your answer what resource you used.

1. You are organizing a tour to New York City. The group leader tells you that participants would like to see a Broadway show. What is the average cost of a theater ticket (orchestra seat) for a hit musical? Are any group rates available?

2. What budget hotel accommodations are available in New York City? List three possibilities and their rates.

3. Does Walt Disney World have any package plans that include admission tickets and on-site hotels? Provide details for one.

# Worksheet 2.6: Looking Back: A Chapter Quiz

_____

Name                                                              Date

**Directions:** Answer the questions in the space provided, or circle the correct answer.

1. Which city or area would have special appeal to its niche travelers?

   _____ History explorers        A. Orlando, Florida

   _____ Gourmets                  B. Hudson River Valley, New York

   _____ Wine tasters              C. Boston, Massachusetts

   _____ Harness-racing fans       D. Camden, Maine

   _____ Windjammer cruisers       E. Newport, Rhode Island

   _____ Theme park lovers         F. Finger Lakes area, New York

   _____ Mansion admirers          G. Saratoga, New York

2. Name a mountain range in each state.

   New Hampshire      _____

   Vermont            _____

   New York           _____

   North Carolina     _____

   Virginia           _____

3. How would you characterize the climate of South Florida?

   _____

4. When is the official hurricane season for the East Coast?

   _____

5. The travelers live in New York City and want to visit a resort and do some gambling. Name two destinations within a few hours' drive.

   _____

   _____

6. Name five home port cities that cruise ships are using along the East Coast.

_____

_____

_____

7. Amber and Maurice are headed to New York City on their honeymoon. They have heard that if they get up early and go to the NBC-TV studios, they stand a chance of getting to wave to the folks back home and be on the *Today* show. Where in the city should they go?

_____

_____

8. Which New Orleans neighborhood is home to Bourbon Street?
   A. Lee Circle
   B. Warehouse Arts District
   C. French Quarter
   D. Carollton

9. Some travelers would like to plan a trip in the eastern United States to try different types of food. Where would you suggest they go?

_____

_____

_____

10. What is the "Run for the Roses," and where does it take place?

_____

_____

11. Some cities roll up their sidewalks at night; others roll them out. The travelers would like a lot of nighttime activity. Where do you think they should go? Give three choices.

_____

_____

12. What are the attractions of Mississippi's Gulf Coast?

_____

_____

# CHAPTER 3

# The Midwest

## ■ Resources

Great Lakes
www.glna.org

Lake cruising
www.greatlakescruising.com

*Midwest Living* (magazine)
www.midwestliving.com

Rail travel
www.amtrak.com

### Arkansas
www.arkansas.com

Hot Springs
www.hotsprings.org

Little Rock
www.littlerock.com

### Illinois
www.enjoyillinois.com

Cahokia Mounds
www.cahokiamounds.com

Chicago
www.choosechicago.com

Springfield
www.visitspringfieldillinois.com

Willis Tower
www.willistower.com

### Indiana
www.tourindiana.com

Bloomington
www.visitbloomington.com

Indianapolis
www.indy.org

### Iowa
www.traveliowa.com

Des Moines
www.seedesmoines.com

### Kansas
www.travelks.com

### Michigan
www.michigan.org

Detroit
www.visitdetroit.com

### Minnesota
www.exploreminnesota.com

Mall of America
www.mallofamerica.com

Minneapolis
www.minneapolis.org

St. Paul
www.visitstpaul.com

## Missouri
www.visitmo.com

Branson
www.explorebranson.com

Gateway Arch
www.gatewayarch.com

Hannibal
www.visithannibal.com

St. Louis
www.explorestlouis.com

## Nebraska
www.visitnebraska.org

Henry Doorly Zoo
www.omahazoo.com

Lincoln
www.lincoln.org

Omaha
www.visitomaha.com

## North Dakota
www.ndtourism.com

## Ohio
www.discoverohio.com

Cincinnati
www.cincyusa.com

Cleveland
www.travelcleveland.com

Columbus
www.columbuscvb.org

Rock and Roll Hall of Fame
rockhall.com

## Oklahoma
www.oktourism.com

Oklahoma City
www.visitokc.com

Tulsa
www.visittulsa.com

## South Dakota
www.travelsd.com

Rapid City
www.rapidcitycvb.com

Sioux Falls
www.siouxfallscvb.com

## Texas
www.traveltexas.com

Austin
www.austintexas.org

Bandera
www.banderacowboycapital.com

Corpus Christi
www.corpuschristi-tx-cvb.org

Dallas
www.visitdallas.com

El Paso
www.elpasocvb.com

Fort Worth
www.fortworth.com

Galveston Island
www.galveston.com

Houston
www.houston-spacecity.com

San Antonio
www.sanantoniovisit.com

## Wisconsin
www.travelwisconsin.com

Madison
www.visitmadison.com

Milwaukee
www.officialmilwaukee.com

# ■ UNESCO World Heritage Sites

For the Midwest, the UNESCO World Heritage List includes the following:

## Cultural Heritage

- Cahokia Mounds State Historic Site, Illinois

## Natural Heritage

None

# ■ Reading Suggestions: The Midwest

- Willa Cather: *O Pioneers!* (1913) and *My Antonia* (1918) are stories she had heard as a child from Swedish immigrants in Nebraska.

- Edna Ferber: *Giant* (1952) is a story of Texas oil, and *Cimarron* (1930), a story of the land rush of 1889 in Oklahoma.

- William Least Heat-Moon: *Blue Highways* (1982) is about a journey on America's back roads.

- James Michener: *Texas* (1985) offers more about the state.

- Upton Sinclair: *The Jungle* (1906) is a novel about Chicago, immigrants, and the meatpacking industry.

- John Steinbeck: *The Grapes of Wrath* (1939) tells of family members forced out of their home in the Oklahoma Dust Bowl and their migration to California.

- Laura Ingalls Wilder: *Little House on the Prairie* (1930s) series contain books about pioneer life and is the basis of the popular TV series.

# Worksheet 3.1: Geography

_____                         _____
Name                                                                      Date

**Directions:** Answer the questions in the space provided.

1. What will the weather in Chicago be like in May?

   _____

2. What were Lewis and Clark looking for?

   _____

   _____

3. Which Great Lake is the only one entirely in the United States?

   _____

4. Texas has water borders on two of its sides. Name the bodies of water.

   _____

   _____

5. Describe the physical characteristics of the land that stretches from the Appalachian Highlands to the Rocky Mountains.

   _____

   _____

   _____

   _____

6. What are tornadoes? Where is Tornado Alley?

   _____

   _____

   _____

# Worksheet 3.2: Itinerary Planning

_____

Name                                                                    Date

You are working for one of the auto clubs. Outline a 7-day driving trip through Texas for a family of four. They plan to go during the children's (ages 10 and 13) spring vacation. They will fly to San Antonio from their home in Chicago and then rent a car at the airport.

# Worksheet 3.3: Answering Questions

_____
Name                                                              Date

**Directions:** How would you respond to travelers who ask the following questions?

1. "I'm a very picky eater. What if I don't like the food on the tour?"

2. "We are taking our children (ages 12 and 14) along on this driving trip to the Badlands. What can they do in addition to seeing the scenery?"

# Worksheet 3.4: Map Review

# Worksheet 3.4: Map Review

Name _____   Date _____

**Directions:** Match the destination with its number on the map. Give the three-letter airport code of the destination or its nearest airport.

| Map Number | | Airport Code |
|---|---|---|
| _____ | Alamo | _____ |
| _____ | Big Bend National Park | _____ |
| _____ | Branson | _____ |
| _____ | Gateway Arch | _____ |
| _____ | Guthrie Theater | _____ |
| _____ | Indiana Dunes National Lakeshore | _____ |
| _____ | Mackinac Island | _____ |
| _____ | Mount Rushmore | _____ |
| _____ | Padre Island | _____ |
| _____ | Rock and Roll Hall of Fame and Museum | _____ |
| _____ | The Loop | _____ |

# Worksheet 3.5: Using Reference Materials

Name                                                       Date

**Directions:** Using available resources, answer the questions in the space provided. Indicate in your answer what resource you used.

1. What is playing in the theaters of Branson?

2. What are some of the activities and promotions presently drawing visitors to Chicago?

3. What is the weather like in Corpus Christi today?

4. How far is the Dallas/Fort Worth Airport from downtown Dallas? Approximately what is the cab or shuttle bus fare?

# Worksheet 3.6: Looking Back: A Chapter Quiz

Name _____  Date _____

## Matching

**Directions:** Match the states with their attractions or cities.

Missouri        Arkansas        Kansas        South Dakota        Oklahoma

Iowa        Texas        Nebraska        North Dakota

1. Lewis and Clark passed through it while exploring the West. Its largest city is Fargo.

   _____

2. It is called the *Gateway to the West*, with Mark Twain country and Branson.

   _____

3. It is the largest of the lower forty-eight. The Rio Grande is part of its southern border with Mexico.

   _____

4. Fertile plains attracted the Amish settlers.

   _____

5. Scotts Bluff is one of its cities, and Buffalo Bill was a prominent citizen.

   _____

6. It is home to the Black Hills and the Badlands.

   _____

7. The Santa Fe and Chisholm Trails pass through. The Eisenhower Library is in Abilene.

   _____

8. The Ozarks are its mountains, and Hot Springs is the place to take a relaxing bath.

   _____

9. It is the home of many Native American tribes and the National Cowboy Hall of Fame.

   _____

## True or False

**Directions:** Circle either True or False.

True        False        1. Lake Erie is the only one of the Great Lakes entirely in the United States.

True        False        2. Tornado Alley includes the states of Texas, Oklahoma, Kansas, Nebraska, and Iowa.

| | | |
|---|---|---|
| True | False | 3. The Ozark-Ouachita Highlands rise in southern Missouri, northwestern Arkansas, and eastern Oklahoma. |
| True | False | 4. Auto racing fans head to Great Bend, Indiana, for the annual 500 race. |
| True | False | 5. Mackinac Island is a summer resort between Lakes Huron and Michigan. |
| True | False | 6. The northern part of Wisconsin is a barren region with few trees. |
| True | False | 7. Frank Lloyd Wright was a famous poet who wrote about Chicago. |
| True | False | 8. Some of Chicago's attractions are the Field Museum of Natural History and Robie House. |
| True | False | 9. The Mall of America is located near the Minneapolis Airport. |
| True | False | 10. Gateway Arch in St. Louis, Missouri, is a monument to westward expansion. |
| True | False | 11. The National Cowboy Hall of Fame and Western Heritage Center is in Oklahoma City. |
| True | False | 12. Nebraska is home to Boot Hill Cemetery and the Eisenhower Library. |

# CHAPTER 4

# The Western States, Alaska, and Hawaii

## ■ Resources

Dude Ranch Association
www.duderanch.org

Rail travel
www.amtrak.com

*Sunset* magazine
www.sunset.com

### Alaska

www.travelalaska.com

Alaska Highway
www.themilepost.com

Alaska Railroad
www.akrr.com

Anchorage
www.anchorage.net

Fairbanks
www.explorefairbanks.com

Iditarod
www.iditarod.com

Juneau
www.traveljuneau.com

White Pass Railroad
www.whitepassrailroad.com

### Arizona

www.arizonaguide.com

Flagstaff
www.flagstaffarizona.org

Grand Canyon
www.nps.gov/grca

Phoenix
www.visitphoenix.com

Scottsdale
www.scottsdalecvb.com

Tucson
www.visittucson.org

## California

www.gocalif.ca.gov

Alcatraz
www.nps.gov/alcatraz

Death Valley
www.nps.gov/deva

Disneyland
www.disneyland. go.com

Golden Gate Bridge
www.goldengatebridge.org

Hearst Castle
www.hearstcastle.org

Los Angeles
www.lacvb.com

Monterey
www.montereyinfo.org

Napa Valley
www.napavalley.com

Palm Springs
www.palmspringsusa.com

San Diego
www.sandiego.org

San Diego Zoo
www.sandiegozoo.org

San Francisco
www.sfvisitor.org

Universal Studios
www.universalstudios.com

Yosemite
www.nps.gov/yose

## Colorado

www.colorado.travel

Aspen
www.aspen-snowmass.com

Breckenridge
www.breckenridge.com

Colorado Ski Country
www.coloradoski.com

Colorado Springs
www.coloradosprings-travel.com

Denver
www.denver.org

Estes Park
www.estesparktravel.com

Gunnison-Crested Butte
www.gunnisoncrestedbutte.com

Steamboat
www.steamboat.com

Vail
www.snow.com

## Hawaii

www.gohawaii.com

Bishop Museum
www.bishopmuseum.org

Dole Plantation
www.dole-plantation.com

Hawaii (the island)
www.bigisland.org

Iolani Palace
www.iolanipalace.org

Lanai
www.visitlanai.net

Maui
www.visitmaui.com

Molokai
www.molokaihawaii.com

Oahu
www.visitoahu.com

## Idaho

www.visitid.com

Boise
www.boise.org

## Montana

www.visitmt.com

## Nevada

www.travelnevada.com

Carson City
www.visitcarsoncity.com

Hoover Dam
www.hooverdamtours.com

Las Vegas
www.lasvegas24hours.com

Las Vegas monorail
www.lvmonorail.com

Reno-Sparks
www.renolaketahoe.com

Tahoe
www.tahoechamber.org

## New Mexico

www.newmexico.org

Albuquerque
www.itsatrip.org

Carlsbad
www.nps.gov/cave

Chaco National Park
www.nps.gov/chcu

Cumbres & Toltec Rail
www.cumbrestoltec.com

Indian Arts and Culture
www.miaclab.org

Indian Pueblo Culture Center
www.indianpueblo.org

Santa Fe
www.santafe.org

Taos
www.taoschamber.com

## Oregon

www.traveloregon.com

American West Steamboat
www.columbiarivercruise.com

Portland
www.travelportland.com

## Utah

www.utahtravel.org

Canyonlands
www.discovermoab.com

Dinosaurland
www.dinoland.com

Salt Lake City
www.visitsaltlake.com

## Washington

www.experiencewashington.com

Seattle
www.seeseattle.org

Space Needle
www.spaceneedle.com

Spokane
www.visitspokane.com

## Wyoming

www.wyomingtourism.org

Cheyenne
www.cheyenne.org

Jackson Hole
www.jacksonholewy.com

Yellowstone
www.nps.gov.yell

# ■ UNESCO World Heritage Sites

For the western states, Alaska, and Hawaii, the UNESCO World Heritage List includes the following:

## Cultural Heritage

- Chaco Culture National Historical Park, New Mexico

- Mesa Verde National Park, Colorado

- Pueblo de Taos, New Mexico

## Natural Heritage

- Carlsbad Caverns National Park, New Mexico

- Grand Canyon National Park, Arizona

- Hawaii Volcanoes National Park, Hawaii

- Olympic National Park, Washington

- Redwood National Park, California

- Waterton-Glacier International Peace Park, Montana

- *Yellowstone National Park, Wyoming

- Yosemite National Park, California

# ■ Reading Suggestions: The Western States, Alaska, and Hawaii

- Stephen E. Ambrose: *Undaunted Courage* (2004) is a historian's account of the Lewis and Clark mission.

- Ben Mezrich: *Bringing Down the House: The Inside Story of Six MIT Students Who Took Vegas for Millions* (2004) is about winning, winning, winning.

- James Michener: *Centennial* (1974), *Hawaii* (1957), and *Alaska* (1988) are sweeping narratives mixing fact and fiction.

- John Steinbeck: *Cannery Row* (1945) and its sequel, *Sweet Thursday* (1954), follow the adventures of workers in a California cannery.

# Worksheet 4.1: Geography

_____

Name                                                                Date

**Directions:** Answer the questions in the space provided.

1. Which city is farther west: Los Angeles, California, or Reno, Nevada?

   _____

2. What is a continental divide?

   _____

3. What are the highest and lowest elevations in the United States? Where are they?

   _____

   _____

4. What is a glacier?

   _____

5. What forces of nature formed the Grand Canyon? In what U.S. state is it located?

   _____

   _____

6. Which mountain ranges run north–south through western Washington and Oregon and most of California?

   _____

7. What is a fault? What is the significance of the one called San Andreas?

   _____

   _____

   _____

8. In what U.S. state does it rain the most?

   _____

# Worksheet 4.2: Itinerary Planning

Name _____ Date _____

You are working for the California Tourist Board. Outline a trip through the state for a family of four departing from Kansas City. The children's ages are 14 and 12. The family enjoys the outdoors but wants some tips for city sightseeing, especially in San Francisco.

# Worksheet 4.3: Answering Questions

---

Name                                                                     Date

**Directions:** How would you respond to travelers in the following situations?

1. You are employed by a tour operator specializing in Las Vegas trips. A phone customer says: "I know there are bargains to be had at hotels and restaurants in Las Vegas and wonder what tips you could offer to help us find the good deals. Is there a value season?"

2. You are working for New Mexico's tourist board. The traveler says: "I plan to take my grandson to New Mexico as a graduation present. We both are interested in Native American culture. Any recommendations?"

3. "My husband and I are going to Oahu for the first time and wonder if there any must-sees and must-dos beyond the usual tourist haunts?"

# Worksheet 4.4: Map Review

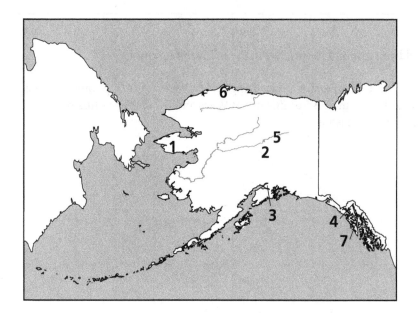

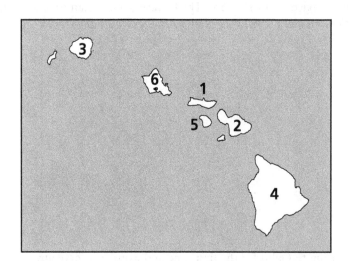

# Worksheet 4.4: Map Review

Name                                                                 Date

**Directions:** Answer the questions in the space provided. Match the destination with its number on the map. Give the three-letter airport code of the destination or of the nearest airport city.

1. **Map Number**                           **Airport Code**

   _____    Anchorage     _____

   _____    Barrow     _____

   _____    Denali     _____

   _____    Fairbanks     _____

   _____    Juneau     _____

   _____    Nome     _____

   _____    Skagway     _____

2. Which points are above the Arctic Circle?

_____

_____

3. Which cities are on the Alaska Panhandle?

_____

_____

4. Match the island with its number on the map of Hawaii. Give the three-letter code of the island's airport.

**Map Number**                           **Airport Code**

   _____    Hawaii     _____

   _____    Kauai     _____

   _____    Lanai     _____

   _____    Maui     _____

   _____    Molokai     _____

   _____    Oahu     _____

# Worksheet 4.5: Using Reference Materials

| | |
|---|---|
| Name | Date |

**Directions:** Answer the questions in the space provided. Indicate in your answer what resource you used.

1. How are the ski conditions in Aspen today?

2. What well-known stars are appearing in Las Vegas this week?

3. What documentation is required from a U.S. citizen who wants to cross the Mexican border at San Diego and spend the day in Tijuana?

4. Name three five-star resorts in or near Phoenix, Arizona.

5. What is the weather like today in Denali?

# Worksheet 4.6: Looking Back: A Chapter Quiz

_____

Name                                                                Date

## Matching

1. **Directions:** Match the city with its sights.

   Albuquerque          Denver          Las Vegas          Los Angeles          Phoenix

   Salt Lake City          San Diego          San Francisco          Santa Fe

   A. Ghirardelli Square, Lombard Street, and Fisherman's Wharf          _____

   B. Taliesin West and Camelback Mountain          _____

   C. The Strip and Hoover Dam          _____

   D. Balboa Park, Cabrillo Monument, and Tijuana          _____

   E. Olvera Street and Gehry's Hall          _____

   F. Art, opera, adobe homes, and pueblos          _____

   G. Molly Brown and LoDo (and Coors, too)          _____

   H. Largest city in New Mexico and famous balloon festival          _____

   I. Temple Square and the Tabernacle          _____

2. **Directions:** Match the state with its description and attractions. Some states are used more than once.

   Idaho          Montana          Oregon          Washington

   A. It is called Big Sky Country and is where Custer
      made his last stand.          _____

   B. It is timber country with the Columbia River Gorge.          _____

   C. The Olympic Peninsula and Mount Saint Helens
      are part of its natural beauty.          _____

   D. The state's cities include Billings, Helena, and Missoula.          _____

   E. Attractions include the Selway-Bitterroot Wilderness
      and the Frank Church River of No Return Wilderness Area.          _____

   F. The state's largest city celebrates the Rose Festival in June.          _____

3. **Directions:** Match the Hawaiian island with its description.

Hawaii　　　　Kauai　　　　Lanai　　　　Maui　　　　Molokai　　　　Oahu

A. Once a pineapple ranch, it is now a low-key resort
   with good golf courses.

_____

B. Once a leper colony, it is now welcoming and peaceful,
   with unspoiled beauty.

_____

C. The largest island, it is known for its active volcanoes.

_____

D. The busiest island, it is home to the Polynesian
   Cultural Center.

_____

E. It is the lushest island, with canyons and cliffs.

_____

F. You can ride a bicycle down its volcano.

_____

## Multiple Choice

**Directions:** Circle the answer to the statement or question.

1. The tallest mountain on the North American continent is
   A. Mount Hood.
   B. Mount McKinley.
   C. Mount Rainier.
   D. Mount Whitney.

2. Which state has the longest coastline?
   A. California
   B. Hawaii
   C. Washington
   D. Alaska

3. What is the fastest-growing metropolitan area in the United States?
   A. Los Angeles
   B. Seattle
   C. Las Vegas
   D. San Diego

4. The sun shines at midnight near the horizon and never sets in northern Alaska during
   A. June.
   B. September.
   C. December.
   D. March.

5. The Alaska Marine Highway is
   A. a system of ferry boats along the coast.
   B. a highway along the coast of the Panhandle.
   C. a cruise ship route through the Inland Passage.
   D. a system of floatplanes that service the state.

# Worksheet 4.6: Looking Back: A Chapter Quiz (continued)

Name                                                       Date

6. Which of the following Alaskan destinations cannot be reached by car?
   A. Fairbanks
   B. Denali
   C. Glacier Bay
   D. Anchorage

7. On which Hawaiian island does it rain the most?
   A. Oahu
   B. Hawaii
   C. Kauai
   D. Maui

# CHAPTER 5

# Canada

## ■ Resources

The Canadian government maintains tourism offices in several U.S. cities, and through the offices and provincial Web sites, information is readily available.

### Canada
www.canadatourism.com

National parks
www.pc.gc.ca

VIA Rail Canada
www.viarail.ca

### Alberta
www.travelalberta.com

Banff National Park
www.banfflakelouise.com

Calgary Stampede
www.calgarystampede.com

Jasper National Park
www.jaspercanadianrockies.com

West Edmonton Mall
www.westedmontonmall.com

### British Columbia
www.hellobc.com

BC ferries
www.bcferries.bc.ca

BC skiing
www.bcskiing.com

Vancouver
www.tourismvancouver.com

Victoria
www.tourismvictoria.com

### Manitoba
www.travelmanitoba.com

### New Brunswick
www.gov.nb.ca/tourism

### Newfoundland/Labrador
www.gov.nf.ca/tourism

### Northwest Territories
www.gov.nt.ca

### Nova Scotia
www.gov.ns.ca/tourism

### Nunavut
www.nunatour.nt.ca

## Ontario
www.travelnx.com

CN Tower
www.cntower.ca

National Gallery of Canada
www.nationalgallery.ca

Niagara Falls
www.tourismniagara.com

Toronto
www.torontotourism.com

## Prince Edward Island
www.peiplay.com

## Québec
www.bonjourquebec.com

Laurentians
www.laurentians.com

Montréal
www.tourism-montreal.org

Mount Tremblant
www.tremblant.ca

## Saskatchewan
www.sasktourism.com

## Yukon
www.touryukon.com

Kluane National Park
www.parkscan.harbour.com/
kluane

# ■ UNESCO World Heritage Sites

For Canada, the UNESCO World Heritage List includes the following:

## Cultural Heritage

- Anthony Island, British Columbia
- Head-Smashed-in-Buffalo Jump, Alberta
- Historic area, Québec
- L'Anse aux Meadows Historic Park, Newfoundland
- Lunenburg Old City, Nova Scotia

## Natural Heritage

- Canadian Rocky Mountains Parks (Banff and Jasper), British Columbia
- Dinosaur Provincial Park, Alberta
- Gros Morne National Park, Newfoundland
- Miquasha Park, Québec
- Nahanni National Park, Northwest Territories
- Waterton-Glacier International Peace Park, Alberta
- Wood Buffalo National Park, Northwest Territories/Alberta

# ■ Reading Suggestions: Canada

- Ken Follett: *Night over Water* (1992). is a thriller set in 1939 on a Pan Am Clipper's flight from England to America, with stops in Canada for history, romance, and adventure.

- Lucy Maud Montgomery: *Anne of Green Gables* and its sequels contain memories of the author's childhood on Prince Edward Island.

- Howard Norman: *My Famous Evening: Nova Scotia Sojourns, Diaries & Preoccupations* (2004) tells of haunted houses, ocean birds, and the mysteries of coves, storms, and lives spent close to the sea.

- Robert William Service: He is known as "the bard of the Yukon" for such poems as "The Shooting of Dan McGrew," from his collection titled *Song of a Sourdough* (1907).

# Worksheet 5.1: Geography

Name _____ Date _____

**Directions:** Answer the questions in the space provided.

1. How does permafrost affect any settlement built on it?

   _____

   _____

2. At what time of year should travelers expect to find 24 hours of daylight when they visit a destination in northern Canada?

   _____

3. What is the Canadian Shield?

   _____

   _____

   _____

4. Which Canadian town was chosen by Marconi for his first transatlantic radio transmission? Why did he choose it?

   _____

   _____

   _____

5. Would you recommend the beaches of Prince Edward Island to a family from Pennsylvania seeking a warm-water vacation in July? Justify your answer.

   _____

   _____

   _____

6. You are helping some downhill skiers choose a vacation destination sometime next February. They are trying to decide between a resort in the Laurentians and one in the Rockies. What do you know that might be of help to them?

   _____

   _____

   _____

7. What kind of weather should travelers expect for their trip to the Calgary Stampede?

_____

_____

8. What is the St. Lawrence Seaway?

_____

_____

9. Which is the deepest lake in North America, and where is it located?

_____

10. What is Nunavut?

_____

_____

_____

# Worksheet 5.2: Itinerary Planning: Eastern Canada

Name                                                                                          Date

Sam and Mary Champlain from Louisiana are interested in exploring their French roots. They have about 10 days in August to do so. Grandma Champlain has told Sam that the family came from the town of St. Andrews, New Brunswick, on Passamaquoddy Bay. How would you route them to New Brunswick from Louisiana? How will they get around when they get there? Where will they stay? What is there to see in the area?

# Worksheet 5.3: Answering Questions

Name                                                       Date

**Directions:** How would you respond to travelers who ask the following questions?

1. "We don't speak French. Will we have language difficulties in Québec?"

2. "We are from New England. How does the scenery of western Canada differ from that of the Laurentian Mountains, where we go each year to ski?"

# Worksheet 5.4: Map Review

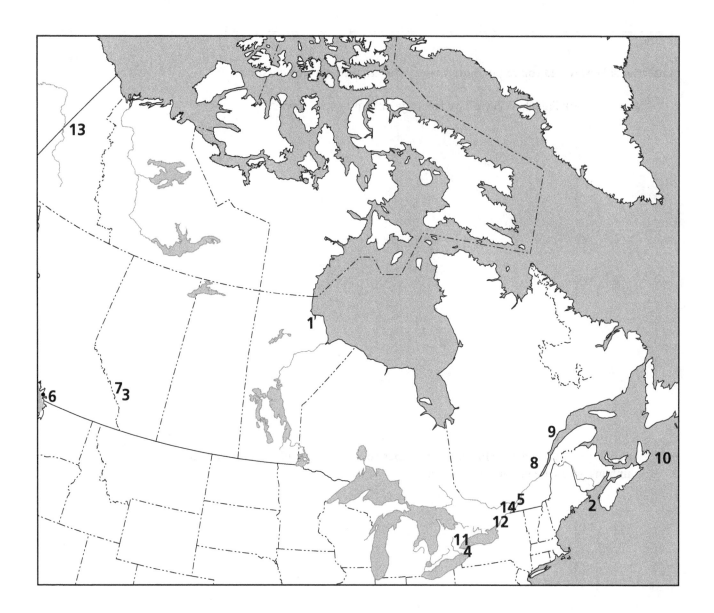

# Worksheet 5.4: Map Review

_____
Name                                                      Date

**Directions:** Match the destination with its number on the map. Give the three-letter airport code of the destination or of the nearest airport.

| Map Number | Destination | Airport Code |
|---|---|---|
| _____ | Bay of Fundy | _____ |
| _____ | Laurentians | _____ |
| _____ | Montréal | _____ |
| _____ | Cabot Trail | _____ |
| _____ | Churchill and polar bears | _____ |
| _____ | Thousand Islands | _____ |
| _____ | Toronto | _____ |
| _____ | Lake Louise | _____ |
| _____ | Ottawa | _____ |
| _____ | Niagara Falls | _____ |
| _____ | Calgary | _____ |
| _____ | Dawson | _____ |
| _____ | Saguenay Fjord | _____ |
| _____ | Vancouver | _____ |
| _____ | L'Anse aux Meadows National Historic Park | _____ |

**Bonus Question:** What is the name of the huge body of water in the middle of Canada that almost bisects the country?

_____

# Worksheet 5.5: Itinerary Planning: Western Canada

Name _____   Date _____

Mr. and Mrs. Lee and their two children, ages 8 and 10, would like your help in planning a driving trip through western Canada. Home for the Lees is San Francisco. What do you suggest?

# Worksheet 5.6: Using Reference Materials

Name _____        Date _____

**Directions:** Using available resources, answer the questions in the space provided. Indicate in your answer what resource you used.

1. What documentation must U.S. leisure travelers have to visit Canada?

    _____

    _____

2. If you exchange U.S. $100 for Canadian money, how many Canadian dollars will you receive?

    _____

3. Will the luxury-loving traveler be happy with accommodations in Montréal? Suggest two hotels.

    _____

    _____

4. The travelers are planning a weekend in Toronto and would like to go when something special is playing in the theaters. What would you suggest?

    _____

    _____

5. Name three tour operators offering motorcoach tours of the Canadian Rockies.

    _____

    _____

    _____

6. What time of year does VIA Rail Canada's cross-country train service operate? How would you make a reservation?

    _____

7. What is the admission fee for Toronto's CN Tower?

    _____

8. A rafting trip down the Alsek River in Kluane National Park and Reserve allows visitors to view the wildlife (including grizzly bears, Dahl sheep, and golden eagles) and glaciers along the way. Permits for rafting on this Canadian Heritage river are strictly limited to one departure per day. How can you help some travelers arrange their trip?

    _____

# Worksheet 5.7: Looking Back: A Chapter Quiz

_____          _____
Name                                                                     Date

**Directions:** Answer the questions in the space provided, or circle the correct answer.

1.  What benefits does the landscape of Canada have for tourism?

    _____

    _____

    _____

    _____

2.  Which is Canada's largest east coast port?

    _____

3.  Does Canada permit gambling?

    _____

4.  Why do they speak French in Québec?

    _____

    _____

5.  What was the Klondike gold rush?

    _____

    _____

6.  What is meant by the term _underground city_? What city has a famous one? Why is the concept a particularly good one for a Canadian city?

    _____

    _____

    _____

7.  In terms of latitude, Vancouver is closest to
    A. Tokyo, Japan.
    B. Brussels, Belgium.
    C. Lisbon, Portugal.
    D. Stockholm, Sweden.

8. Match the attraction on the left with its location on the right.

_____ Cabot Trail                  A. Toronto

_____ Athabasca Glacier            B. Calgary

_____ Gastown                      C. Vancouver Island

_____ Rushing tides                D. Québec City

_____ Shakespearean Festival       E. Winnipeg

_____ Plains of Abraham            F. Vancouver

_____ CN Tower                     G. Cape Breton Island

_____ Folklorama                   H. Stratford

_____ Stampede                     I. Icefields Centre

_____ Butchart Gardens             J. Bay of Fundy

# CHAPTER 6

# Bermuda and the West Indies

## ■ Resources

Because the choice of a hotel or cruise line is central to satisfaction with an island vacation, hotel guides, tour operators, Web sites, and industry networking become important resources. Choosing accommodations by price alone can ruin a vacation.

### Cruise Lines

Official Cruise Guide
www.officialcruiseguide.com

Azamara Club Cruises
www.cruisingpower.com

Carnival Cruise Lines
www.carnival.com

Celebrity Cruises
www.celebrity.com

Costa Cruise Lines
www.costacruises.com

Crystal Cruises
www.crystalcruises.com

Cunard Line
www.cunardline.com

Disney Cruise Line
www.disneycruise.com

Holland America Line
www.hollandamerica.com

Moorings (yacht charters)
www.moorings.com

Nicholson's Yachts
www.cnconnect.com

Norwegian Cruise Line
www.ncl.com

Oceania Cruises
www.oceaniacruises.com

Princess Cruises
www.princess.com

Regent Seven Seas
www.cruisesregentsevenseas.com

Royal Caribbean International
www.cruisingpower.com

Seabourn Cruise Line
www.seabourn.com

Silversea Cruises
www.silversea.com

### Resorts

Beaches
www.beaches.com

Breezes
www.superclubs.com

Club Med
www.clubmed.com

Couples
www.couples.com

Hedonism
www.superclubs.com

Sandals
sandals.com

## Islands

**Anguilla**
www.anguilla-vacation.com

**Antigua and Barbuda**
www.antigua-barbuda.org

**Aruba**
www.aruba.com

**Bahamas**
www.bahamas.com

Atlantis Resort
www.atlantis.com

Harbour Island
www.myharbourisland.com

UNEXSO
www.unexso.com

**Barbados**
www.barbados.org

**Bermuda**
www.bermudatourism.com

**Bonaire**
www.infobonaire.org

**British Virgin Islands**
www.bvitouristboard.com

**Cayman Islands**
www.caymanislands.ky

Turtle Farm
www.turtle.ky

**Curaçao**
www.curacao-tourism.com

**Dominica**
www.dominca.dm

**Dominican Republic**
www.domincanrepublic.com

**Granada**
www.granadagrenadines.org

**Guadeloupe**
www.frenchcaribbean.com

**Haiti**
www.haititourisme.com

**Jamaica**
www.visitjamaica.com

**Martinique**
www.martinique.org

**Montserrat**
www.visitmontserrat.com

**Puerto Rico**
www.gotopuertorico.com

**Saba**
www.sabatourism.com

**St. Barthélemy**
www.st-barths.com

**St. Eustatius (Statia)**
www.statiatourism.com

**St. Kitts and Nevis**
www.stkitts-tourism.com
www.nevisisland.com

**St. Lucia**
www.stlucia.org

**St. Maarten**
www.st-maarten.com

**St. Martin**
www.st-martin.org

**St. Vincent and Grenadines**
www.svgtourism.com

**Trinidad and Tobago**
www.visittnt.com

**Turks and Caicos**
www.turksandcaicostourism.com

**U.S. Virgin Islands**
www.usvitourism.vi

# ■ UNESCO World Heritage Sites

For Bermuda and the West Indies, the UNESCO World Heritage List includes the following:

## Cultural Heritage

- Brimstone Hill Fortress National Park, St. Kitts and Nevis
- First coffee plantation, Cuba
- La Citadelle, Sans Souci, and Ramiers, Haiti
- La Fortaleza and San Juan historic area, Puerto Rico
- Old Town Havana, Cuba
- Santiago de Cuba, San Pedro de la Roca Castle, Cuba
- St. George town and fortifications, Bermuda
- Santo Domingo colonial city, Dominican Republic
- Trinidad and Valley de los Ingenios, Cuba
- Vitales Valley, Cuba
- Willemstad historic area, Curaçao

## Natural Heritage

- Morne Trois Pitons National Park, Dominica
- Parque Nacional Desembarco de Granma, Cuba

# ■ Reading Suggestions: Bermuda and the West Indies

- Conrad Allen: In *Murder on the Caronia* (2003), ship detectives on Cunard Line's classic old ships solve mysteries at sea. Other books by the same author are *Murder on the Lusitania*, *Murder on the Mauretania*, and *Murder on the Minnesota*.
- Ian Fleming (1908–1964): His spy thrillers featuring James Bond include many Caribbean islands. His former home on Jamaica is a tourist attraction.
- John Grisham: *The Firm* (1991) is a thriller partly set in the Cayman Islands.
- Aarona Booker Kohlman: *Under Tin Roofs* (1993)is a memoir of the author's childhood in the Cayman Islands.
- V. S. Naipaul: *A House for Mr. Biswas* (1961) is a Caribbean classic, written by a Trinidadian novelist, travel writer, and essayist, about a changing Hindu lifestyle.
- Derek Walcott: *Omeros* offers a contemporary odyssey in a Caribbean setting, written by St. Lucia's Nobel Prize–winning poet.
- Herman Wouk: *Don't Stop the Carnival* (1965) is a comedic novel about managing a hotel on a Caribbean island.

# Worksheet 6.1: Geography

Name                                                                    Date

**Directions:** Answer the questions in the space provided. You might have to look back to Chapter 1 for help with some of the answers.

1. What causes waves?

_____

_____

_____

_____

2. How would you describe the climate of Barbados in July?

_____

3. Was Cuba ever part of the United States?

_____

_____

4. What is Bermuda's weather like in January?

_____

5. Is Puerto Rico a state?

_____

6. How did the United States obtain the Virgin Islands?

_____

_____

_____

_____

7. What is the difference between the Greater and Lesser Antilles?

_____

_____

_____

_____

8. Where are the Windward Islands? Name three.

_____

_____

_____

_____

9. Where are the Leeward Islands? Name three.

_____

_____

_____

_____

10. How are coral islands formed? Name two in the Caribbean.

_____

_____

_____

_____

# Worksheet 6.2: Itinerary Planning

Name                                                                                          Date

A typical island vacation usually lasts 1 week. Mr. and Mrs. Manley are heading to a resort near Ocho Rios in Jamaica. What activities other than sitting in the sun are possible?

# Worksheet 6.3: Answering Questions

Name                                                                      Date

**Directions:** How would you respond if travelers asked the following questions?

1. "Isn't a cruise very expensive?"

2. "I've heard that the island is unsafe. Is that true?"

# Worksheet 6.4: Map Review

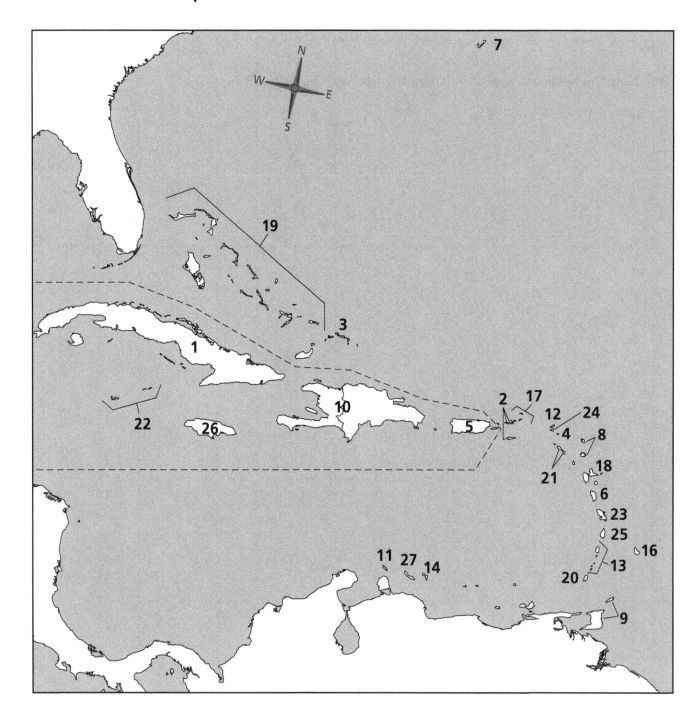

# Worksheet 6.4: Map Review

_____
Name                                                                Date

**Directions:** Find each number on the map, and then fill in the name of the island next to its number. Add the island's airport code or the code of the airport the traveler must use to get there.

| Island Name | Airport Code | Island Name | Airport Code |
|---|---|---|---|
| 1. _____ | | 15. _____ | |
| 2. _____ | | 16. _____ | |
| 3. _____ | | 17. _____ | |
| 4. _____ | | 18. _____ | |
| 5. _____ | | 19. _____ | |
| 6. _____ | | 20. _____ | |
| 7. _____ | | 21. _____ | |
| 8. _____ | | 22. _____ | |
| 9. _____ | | 23. _____ | |
| 10. _____ | | 24. _____ | |
| 11. _____ | | 25. _____ | |
| 12. _____ | | 26. _____ | |
| 13. _____ | | 27. _____ | |
| 14. _____ | | 28. _____ | |

# Worksheet 6.5: Using Reference Materials

Name                                                                      Date

**Directions:** Using available resources, answer the questions in the space provided. Indicate in your answer what resource you used.

1. What are the current documentation requirements for the leisure traveler who wants to visit Barbados?

2. Which islands in the western Caribbean are the ships of Celebrity Cruises visiting this year?

3. Which Jamaican resorts offer all-inclusive vacations?

4. Do ships visiting St. Maarten dock at a pier, or must passengers be tendered to the island?

# Worksheet 6.6: Looking Back: A Chapter Quiz

_____
Name                                                                Date

**Directions:** Fill in the blanks with the correct word or phrase from the list below.

| | | | |
|---|---|---|---|
| Atlantic | Caribbean | leeward | tropical |
| West Indies | windward | from December 15 to April 15 | |
| from June to October | from November to April | golfers | skiers |

1. A large number of islands in the _____ are the exposed
   peaks of an underwater mountain range.

2. The most common type of climate found in the Caribbean is

   _____ .

3. Families with small children seeking calm surf and less exposure to wind should generally seek an island's

   _____ side.

4. Hurricane season in the Caribbean and the East Coast is

   _____ .

5. During winter months (December through April), Bermuda is a popular destination for

   _____ .

6. High season in the Caribbean is _____ .

**Directions:** Name a country in the Caribbean in which each of the following languages is spoken.

7. Spanish        _____

8. French         _____

9. English        _____

10. Papiamento    _____

11. Hindi         _____

**Directions:** Write the answer in each blank.

12. Name four islands known for their excellent scuba-diving facilities.

   _____

   _____

13. Which islands are ideal destinations for those seeking to charter a yacht?

_____

_____

_____

14. Which islands would you recommend to couples seeking an all-inclusive resort?

_____

_____

_____

# CHAPTER 7

# Mexico and Central America

## ■ Resources

Web sites for countries outside the United States are not always in English. Some sites are in the country's official language only. Others give the user a choice of that language or English.

**Belize**
www.travelbelize.org

**Costa Rica**
www.visitcostarica.com

Aerial tram
www.rainforesttram.com

**El Salvador**
www.elsalvadortourism.org

**Guatemala**
www.mayaspirit.com.gt

**Honduras**
www.letsgohonduras.com

**Mexico**
www.visitmexico.com

Baja California
www.visitcabo.com

Cancun
www.cancun.com

Chihuahua Tourism
www.coppercanyon-mexico.com

Mexico City
www.mexicocity.gob.mx

Puerto Vallarta
www.visitpuertovallarta.com

**Nicaragua**
www.intur.gob.ni

**Panama**
www.panamatours.com

# ■ UNESCO World Heritage Sites

For Mexico and Central America, the UNESCO World Heritage List includes the following:

## Cultural Heritage

- Campeche fortified town, Mexico
- Chichén Itzá pre-Hispanic city, Mexico
- Guadalajara Hospicio Cabanas, Mexico
- Guanajuato historic town and mines, Mexico
- Leon Viejo ruins, Nicaragua
- Mexico City historic center, Mexico
- Monte Alban archaeological site and Oaxaca center, Mexico
- Palenque pre-Hispanic city and park, Mexico
- Panama City historic district, Panama
- Parque Nacional Tikal, Guatemala
- Popocatépetl monasteries, Mexico
- Portobelo and San Lorenzo fortifications, Panama
- Puebla historic center, Mexico
- Quiriguá archaeological site, El Salvador
- Sierra de San Francisco rock paintings, Mexico
- Teotihuacán pre-Hispanic city, Mexico
- Uxmal pre-Hispanic city, Mexico
- Xochicalco archaeological site, Mexico
- Xochimilco, Mexico
- Zacatecas historic center, Mexico

## Natural Heritage

- Area de Conservación Guanacaste, Costa Rica
- Barrier reef, Belize
- Cordillera de Talamanca and Parque Internacional La Amistad, Costa Rica/ Panama
- El Vizcaino whale sanctuary, Mexico
- Parque Nacional del Darién, Panama
- Parque Nacional Isla del Coco, Costa Rica
- Parque Nacional Tikal, Guatemala
- *Reserva Biósfera Rio Platano, Honduras
- Reserva Biosfera Sian Ka'an, Mexico

# ■ Reading Suggestions: Mexico and Central America

- Tony Cohan: *On Mexican Time* (2000) is a memoir of the author's family's expatriate life in San Miguel de Alende, Mexico.

- David McCullough: *The Path between the Seas* (1977) contains gripping narrative, scholarly research, and photographic imagery about the Panama Canal.

- James Michener: *Mexico* (1992) is one of his many novels.

- Samuel Shellabarger: In *Captain from Castile* (1945), Cortez meets the Aztecs. This was made into a swashbuckling film.

- Paul Theroux: *The Mosquito Coast* (1982) is a scathing account of a man's attempt to colonize an inhospitable corner of Central America.

# Worksheet 7.1: Geography

Name _____ Date _____

**Directions:** Answer the questions in the space provided, or circle the correct answer.

1. What is the difference between Central America and Latin America?

   _____

   _____

   _____

2. Which Mexican peninsula separates the Gulf of Mexico from the Caribbean Sea?
   A. Baja
   B. Las Playas
   C. Yucatán
   D. Nicoya

3. Which river forms part of Mexico's border with the United States?
   A. Tepalcatepec
   B. Rio Grande
   C. Panuco
   D. Atengo

4. Mexico has _____ states and 1 federal territory.
   A. 28
   B. 31
   C. 32
   D. 34

5. The Copper Canyon is in Mexico's
   A. south.
   B. north.
   C. east.
   D. west.

6. Many of Mexico's best golf courses are found in
   A. Chihuahua.
   B. Copper Canyon.
   C. Los Cabos.
   D. Colonial Cities.

7. Which of the following is considered a Mexican colonial city, not a resort?
   A. Huatulco
   B. Ixtapa
   C. Guadalajara
   D. Acapulco

8. The largest country in Central America is
   A. Nicaragua.
   B. Guatemala.
   C. Costa Rica.
   D. Panama.

9. The world's second-longest barrier reef is located off the coast of
   A. Costa Rica.
   B. Honduras.
   C. Panama.
   D. Belize.

10. When entering from the Pacific, ships sailing through the Panama Canal sail
    A. northwest.
    B. southeast.
    C. northeast.
    D. southwest.

11. English is the official language in
    A. Costa Rica.
    B. El Salvador.
    C. Belize.
    D. Honduras.

# Worksheet 7.2: Itinerary Planning

Name                                                                                    Date

The Riveras are fascinated by Mexican archaeology. Outline a 10-day trip for them to the Mayan sites of the Yucatán Peninsula.

# Worksheet 7.3: Answering Questions

Name                                                                    Date

**Directions:** How would you respond to travelers who asked the following questions?

1. "My 20-year-old grandson is planning to travel alone to Mexico to visit a friend in Ciudad Ayala. He speaks fluent Spanish but has not traveled in a foreign country. We've heard that Mexico has a lot of crime and want to help him have a safe, enjoyable trip. What do you suggest?"

2. "What do you know about Mexico's Copper Canyon, including the best time to visit, interesting things to see, and available tours?"

# Worksheet 7.4: Map Review

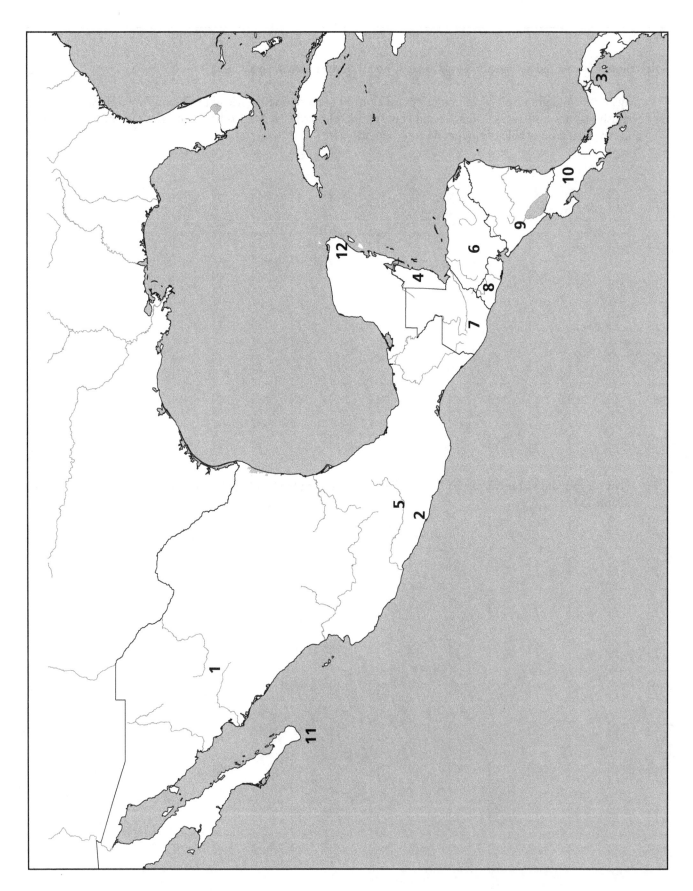

# Worksheet 7.4: Map Review

Name _____ Date _____

**Directions:** Match the destination listed below with its number on the map. Give the three-letter airport code of the destination or of the nearest airport.

| Map Number | | Airport Code |
|---|---|---|
| _____ | Acapulco | _____ |
| _____ | Belmopan | _____ |
| _____ | Cancún | _____ |
| _____ | Copper Canyon | _____ |
| _____ | Guatemala City | _____ |
| _____ | Los Cabos | _____ |
| _____ | Managua | _____ |
| _____ | Panama City | _____ |
| _____ | San José, Costa Rica | _____ |
| _____ | San Salvador | _____ |
| _____ | Taxco | _____ |
| _____ | Tegucigalpa | _____ |

**Bonus Question:** What is the name of the body of water between Baja California and the mainland of Mexico?

_____

# Worksheet 7.5: Using Reference Materials

Name                                                                    Date

**Directions:** Using available resources, answer the questions in the space provided. Indicate in your answer what resource you used.

1. What health hazards, if any, does the Centers for Disease Control report in Belize?

2. Does the U.S. State Department have any advisories for Central American countries? If so, what are the advisories, and which countries are affected?

3. What are the documentation requirements for a single parent who wants to take a child along on a vacation to Mexico?

4. What can you find out about diving conditions in the Bay Islands of Honduras?

5. What tour companies offer rafting trips in Costa Rica? On what rivers?

# Worksheet 7.6: Looking Back: A Chapter Quiz

Name _____          Date _____

**Directions:** Answer the questions in the space provided.

1. Match the civilizations with their areas.

    _____ Aztec              A. Yucatán and Central America

    _____ Olmec              B. Mexico City

    _____ Maya               C. North of Mexico City

    _____ Toltec             D. East coast of Mexico

**Directions:** Answer the following questions.

2. In which Central American country are 90 percent of the people of almost pure European descent?

    _____

3. Is Baja California part of the United States? If not, to which country does it belong?

    _____

    _____

4. Name three important dive destinations in Mexico and Central America.

    _____

    _____

    _____

5. The travelers would like a vacation in the sun, with good beaches and active nightlife. Name three destinations that would suit them.

    _____

    _____

    _____

6. The travelers would like to visit archaeological sites tied to the Mayan culture. Name three in Mexico or Central America.

    _____

    _____

    _____

# CHAPTER 8

# South America and Antarctica

## ◼ Resources

Lindblad Expeditions
www.expeditions.com

### Argentina
www.turismo.gov.ar

Buenos Aires
www.buenosaires.gov.ar

### Bolivia
www.bolivia-usa.org

### Brazil
www.braziltourism.org

### Chile
www.visitchile.org

Easter Island (Rapa Nui)
www.sernatur.cl

### Colombia
www.colombiaemb.org

### Ecuador
www.vivecuador.com

Falkland Islands
www.tourism.org.fk

Galápagos Islands
www.parquegalapagos.org.ec

### Peru
www.peru.org.pe

Machu Picchu
www.machupicchuperu.com

# ■ UNESCO World Heritage Sites

For South America, the UNESCO World Heritage List includes the following:

## Cultural Heritage

- Brasilia, Brazil
- Caracas university campus, Venezuela
- Cartegena port, fortress, and monuments, Colombia
- *Chan Chan archaeological area, Peru
- Chavin archaeological site, Peru
- Chiquitos Jesuit missions, Bolivia
- Colonia del Sacramento historic center, Uruguay
- Cordoba Jesuit block and estancias, Argentina
- Cuenca historic center, Ecuador
- Cuzco old city, Peru
- Diamantina historic center, Brazil
- El Fuerte de Sanmaipata, Bolivia
- Jesús and Trinidad Jesuit missions, Paraguay
- Lima historic center, Peru
- Maria Mayor Guarani Jesuit missions, Argentina
- Nazca geoglyphs and Pampas de Juma, Peru (Arequipa historic center, Peru)
- Olinda historic center, Brazil
- Parque Arqueológico San Agustín, Colombia
- Potosí, Bolivia
- Quitó old city, Ecuador
- Salvador de Bahia historic center, Brazil
- Santuario Histórica Machu Picchu, Peru
- São Miguel Jesuit mission ruins, Brazil
- Sucre historic city, Bolivia
- Tiwanaku pre-Hispanic city, Bolivia

## Natural Heritage

- Central Surinam Nature Reserve, Surinam
- Discovery Coast Atlantic forest reserves, Brazil
- Pantanal conservation area, Brazil
- Parque Nacional Canaima, Venezuela
- Parque Nacional de Iguazú, Argentina
- Parque Nacional del Manú, Peru
- *Parque Nacional do Iguaçu, Brazil

- Parque Nacional Galápagos, Galápagos Islands

- Parque Nacional Huascarán, Peru

- Parque Nacional Jaú, Brazil

- Parque Nacional Los Glaciares, Argentina

- Parque Nacional Los Katios, Colombia

- Parque Nacional Noel Kempff Mercado, Bolivia

- Parque Nacional Rio Abiseo, Peru

- *Parque Nacional Sangay, Ecuador

- Parque Nacional Serra da Capivara, Brazil

- Parque Nacional Taiampaya & Provincial Ischigualasto, Argentina

- Peninsula Valdés, Argentina

- Santuario Histórico Machu Picchu, Peru

- Southeast Atlantic forest reserves, Brazil

# ■ Reading Suggestions: South America and Antarctica

- Isabel Allende: She wrote *House of the Spirits* (1981). Allende, a Chilean novelist, short-story writer, and journalist, was touted as the first major female figure of Latin American fiction.

- Hiram Bingham: He wrote *Lost City of the Incas: The Story of Machu Picchu and Its Builders* (1972).

- A. B. Daniel: *Incas—The Gold of Cuzco* (2002) is a trilogy about conquistadors and natives.

- Charles Darwin: *Zoology of the Voyage of the Beagle* (1840) was written after his return from his expedition to the South American coast and Australia.

- Ariel Dorfman: *Desert Memories: Journeys through the Chilean North* (2004) recounts the travels of this Chilean playwright, poet, and novelist into the desert, a land with a tormented history.

- Sir Arthur Conan Doyle: The creator of Sherlock Holmes, he wrote the novel *Lost World* (1912) set in the unexplored mountains of Venezuela, a story about dinosaurs roaming on a tepui's isolated roof.

- Pablo Neruda (1904–1973): This Chilean poet was awarded the Nobel Prize for literature in 1971.

- Antonio Skármeta: *The Postman of Neruda* (1987) was inspiration for the film *Il Postino*.

- Paul Theroux: *The Old Patagonia Express* (1979) tells of a trip from Boston to the tip of South America by train.

- Errol Lincoln Uys: *Brazil* (1986) is a novel of the discovery of Brazil.

# Worksheet 8.1: Geography

Name _____ Date _____

**Directions:** Answer the questions in the space provided.

1. Which is farther east: Santiago, Chile, or Miami, Florida?

   _____

2. Which river carries more water than any other in the world?

   _____

3. What is the world's tallest waterfall, and where can travelers find it?

   _____

4. What are the name and location of the world's highest navigable lake?

   _____

5. What is the Strait of Magellan?

   _____

6. What and where is the Atacama?

   _____

7. What country owns Easter Island? How do you get there?

   _____

8. Which South American country has yet to gain its independence?

   _____

9. Where is Devil's Island? To whom does it belong?

   _____

10. Which is the largest city in the Amazon basin?

    _____

11. Which is the world's highest capital city?

    _____

12. Which is the world's southernmost city?

    _____

13. What is the Pan American Highway? What is its route? If you worked for a car-rental firm in Peru, would you recommend the road to drivers?

_____

_____

_____

_____

14. Mount Erebus is a volcano on which continent?

_____

# Worksheet 8.2: Itinerary Planning

Name                                                                     Date

You work for the U.S. State Department and have been given the task of planning the logistics of a business trip for Ricardo Reyes to Santiago, Chile, in August. Mr. Reyes lives in Washington, D.C., and travels on a diplomatic passport. Does he need other documentation? How will you route him? He expects to be in Chile for about 6 weeks, work at the embassy in the city, and have free time on weekends. What suggestions do you have to help him enjoy his trip?

# Worksheet 8.3: Answering Questions

Name                                                                    Date

**Directions:** How would you respond to travelers who asked the following questions?

1. "Rio at Carnival time sounds exciting, but it's such a long trip. Is it worth the trouble?"

2. "What about street crime in Rio?"

# Worksheet 8.4: Map Review

# Worksheet 8.4: Map Review

_____

Name                                                                  Date

**Directions:** Match the destination with its number on the map. Give the three-letter airport code of the destination or of the nearest airport.

| Map Number | | Airport Code |
|---|---|---|
| _____ | Angel Falls | _____ |
| _____ | Buenos Aires | _____ |
| _____ | Cartagena | _____ |
| _____ | Galápagos Islands | _____ |
| _____ | Iguazú Falls | _____ |
| _____ | La Paz | _____ |
| _____ | Lake Titicaca | _____ |
| _____ | Lima | _____ |
| _____ | Manaus | _____ |
| _____ | Montevideo | _____ |
| _____ | Quito | _____ |
| _____ | Rio de Janeiro | _____ |
| _____ | Santiago | _____ |
| _____ | Tierra del Fuego | _____ |

**Bonus Question:** Which South American countries are crossed by the equator?

_____

_____

# Worksheet 8.5: Using Reference Materials

---

Name                                                                    Date

**Directions:** Using available resources, answer the questions in the space provided. Indicate in your answer what resource you used.

1. The Cabrals are planning to visit Rio to see the Carnival festivities. They will stay a week. What are Brazil's documentation requirements for leisure travelers from the United States?

2. From Rio, they would like to make a day trip to Iguazú Falls. Is it possible?

3. What health precautions does the Centers for Disease Control recommend for someone visiting the Amazon rain forest?

4. Ms. Betty Atahualpa has a 2-week vacation coming up this year. She would like to fulfill a dream and see the Inca ruins at Machu Picchu. She just received a tax refund of $2,500. Does she have enough funds for the trip?

# Worksheet 8.6: Looking Back: A Chapter Quiz

Name _____ Date _____

**Directions:** Answer the questions in the space provided.

1. How does the land surface of South America resemble that of North America?

_____

_____

2. What mountain range runs along the western coast of South America?

_____

3. Name South America's highest mountain. Which country claims it?

_____

4. How does a rain forest differ from a jungle?

_____

_____

_____

_____

5. What are the Pampas? Which country has the largest?

_____

_____

6. What is the name of the cold current that flows off South America's Pacific coastline?

_____

7. What is the language of Brazil?

_____

8. Which of the Galápagos Islands is the site of the airport?

_____

9. When is high season in the Galápagos?

_____

10. What city was the center of the Inca empire?

_____

11. How do you get to Machu Picchu?

_____

_____

_____

_____

12. What is the best time of year to take a cruise around Cape Horn?

_____

13. What are geoglyphs? Give an example in South America.

_____

_____

14. Which South American cities are departure ports for expedition cruises to Antarctica?

_____

_____

_____

# CHAPTER 9

# The British Isles

## ◼ Resources

VisitBritain is the national tourist office for England, Wales, Scotland, and Northern Ireland, although each division has its own tourist board. The Irish Tourist Board (Bord Failte) fills the function for the Republic of Ireland. When requesting information, you should be as specific as possible.

One of VisitBritain's many publications is *Movie Map*, featuring locations in England, Scotland, and Wales that have been backdrops in films, including the *Harry Potter* sites.

### England

www.visitbritain.com

Albert Dock
www.albertdock.com

Bath/Roman baths
www.romanbaths.co.uk

Big Ben and Parliament
www.parliament.uk

British Museum
www.thebritishmuseum.ac.uk

British Performing Arts
www.whatsonstage.com

Britrail
www.britrail.com

Canterbury Cathedral
www.canterbury-cathedral.org

Castle Howard
www.castlehoward.co.uk

Docklands Museum
www.museumindocklands.org.uk

Eurostar
www.raileurope.com

Hadrian's Wall Museum
www.hadrians-wall.org

Hampton Court Palace
www.hrp.org.uk

Harrods
www.harrods.com

Hotelboating
www.hotelboating.co.uk

Inland Waterway Cruises
www.bargeholidayuk.com

London
www.visitlondon.com

London Eye
www.ba-londoneye.com

London Pass
www.londonpass.com

London theater
www.londontheatre.co.uk

London Underground
www.thetube.com

National Trust Properties
www.nationaltrust.org.uk

Royal Pavilion/Brighton
www.royalpavilion.brighton.co.uk

St. Paul's Cathedral
www.stpauls.co.uk

Salisbury Cathedral
www.salisburycathedral.org.uk

Shakespeare Houses
www.Shakespeare.org.uk

Stonehenge
www.stonehengemasterplan.org

Stratford-upon-Avon
www.shakespearecountry.co.uk

Tate Britain
www.tate.org.uk/britain

Tate Modern
www.tate.org.uk/modern

Victoria & Albert Museum
www.vam.ac.uk

Warwick Castle
www.warwick-castle.co.uk

Westminster Abbey
www.Westminster-abbey.org

Wimbledon tennis
www.wimbledon.org

Windsor Castle
www.the-royal-collections.org.uk

Yorkshire
www.ytb.org.uk

## Northern Ireland
www.ni-tourism.com

Belfast
www.gotobelfast.com

Causeway Coast and Antrim
www.causewaycoastandglens.com

## Republic of Ireland
www.tourismireland.com

Blarney Castle
www.blarneycastle.ie

Bunratty Castle
www.shannonheritagetrade.com

Dublin
www.visitdublin.com

Guinness Storehouse
www.guinness.com

Irish Country Hotels
www.irishcountryhotels.com

Irish farm holidays
www.irishfarmholidays.com

## Scotland
www.holiday.scotland.net

Edinburgh Castle
www.historic-scotland.gov.uk

Edinburgh Festival
www.eif.co.uk

Scottish castle hotels
www.scotlandsheritagehotels.co.uk

## Wales
www.tourism.wales.gov.uk

Brecon Beacons
www.breconbeacons.org

Caernarfon Castle
www.cadw.wales.gov.uk

Eisteddfod Festivals
www.eisteddfod.com

Snowdonia National Park
www.eryri-npa.gov.uk

Unique properties
www.welshrarebits.co.uk

# ■ UNESCO World Heritage Sites

For the British Isles, the UNESCO World Heritage List includes the following:

## Cultural Heritage

- Bath, England
- Blaenavon industrial landscape, Wales
- Blenheim Palace, England
- Brú Na Bóinne archaeological site at the bend of the Boyne River, Ireland
- Caernarfon Castle, Wales
- Canterbury Cathedral, England
- Durham castle and cathedral, England
- Edinburgh old and new towns
- Hadrian's Wall, England/Scotland
- Ironbridge Gorge, England
- Maritime Greenwich, England
- Orkney archaeological site, Scotland
- Skellig Michael monastic complex, Ireland
- Stonehenge, Avebury, and other megalithic sites, England
- Studley Royal Park and Fountains Abbey, England
- Westminster Abbey and Palace, England

## Natural Heritage

- Giants' Causeway, Northern Ireland
- St. Kilda, Scotland

# ■ Reading Suggestions: The British Isles

Jane Austen once said, "A reader in possession of a good book gains further pleasure from knowing where the author lived, loved, and found inspiration." Her statement inspires literary tours. Tourist centers often have information about authors who lived in their areas and lists of related events.

- R. D. Blackmore: *Lorna Doone, A Romance of Exmoor* (1869) is set in 17th-century Devonshire.
- Charlotte, Emily, and Anne Brontë: Charlotte's *Jane Eyre* (1847) and Emily's *Wuthering Heights* (1847) are considered romance classics.
- Ken Follett: *Pillars of the Earth* (1990) and its sequel, *World Without End* (2007), are the story of the building of a medieval cathedral and a town.

- Winston Graham: He wrote the *Poldark* novels (1945–2002), adventure and romance among 18th-century Cornwall's tin mines.

- Daphne du Maurier: *Rebecca* (1938), *Jamaica Inn* (1936), and *Frenchman's Creek* (1941) offer melodrama, romance, Cornish scenery, and history.

- Thomas Hardy: He wrote eleven Dorsetshire novels (1871–1895), inspiration for countless films.

- James Herriot: *All Creatures Great and Small* (1974), stories of a veterinarian working in the Yorkshire dales, was made into a BBC television series.

- Edward Rutherfurd: He wrote *London* (1997), a story of the city; *Sarum* (1987), based on the history of Salisbury and its cathedral; *The Forest* (2000), a tale of English heritage; and *The Princes of Ireland: The Dublin Saga* (2004), Irish history from the Druids to Henry VIII.

- Leon Uris: *Trinity* (1976) covers a period of Irish history.

- T. H. White: *The Once and Future King* (1958) is about the Arthurian legend.

# Worksheet 9.1: Geography

Name _____ Date _____

**Directions:** Answer the questions in the space provided.

1. How would you describe the landscape of the British Isles?

   _____

   _____

2. What makes the White Cliffs of Dover white? What is the geographic term for the chalk and limestone hills that cross the land and form the cliffs?

   _____

   _____

3. Name England's three main land regions.

   _____

   _____

   _____

4. Describe a moor. Where are most of England's moors found?

   _____

   _____

5. Identify Scotland's principal land regions.

   _____

   _____

6. What is a firth? Name two.

   _____

   _____

   _____

7. What is a loch? Where are they found? Which is Scotland's best-known loch?

   _____

   _____

   _____

8. If travelers want to fish during a visit to the beautiful lakes and rivers of Great Britain, what advance inquiries should they make?

_____

_____

_____

_____

9. What type of niche travelers do the rugged mountains of Wales especially attract?

_____

_____

_____

_____

10. What is Ireland's western coastline known for?

_____

_____

11. What is "turf"?

_____

_____

12. How would you describe the climate of the British Isles? What sort of clothes would you recommend to someone planning a golf trip to Ireland?

_____

_____

_____

13. Why is the landscape of Wales and Ireland so green?

_____

_____

_____

14. What is the time zone of the British Isles?

_____

# Worksheet 9.2: Touring Attractions

_____    _____
Name                                                  Date

Senior citizens and baby boomers account for about 60 percent of the market to the British Isles. Many are repeat visitors. The British Isles can satisfy almost any traveler except those who want to lie on a warm, sunny beach in February. The questions below test your knowledge of basic information about travel in the British Isles.

**Directions:** Answer the questions in the space provided.

1. Visitors who want to shop in stores patronized by royalty should look for the

   _____ displayed above a doorway.

2. _____ mark buildings in London where famous people lived or historic events happened.

3. In London, a display of the Crown Jewels can be found in the

   _____ .

4. Although Windsor Castle has been the sovereign's residence since the time of William the Conqueror, the monarch's London home and the site of a daily pageant at its gates in summer is

   _____ .

5. Where might a traveler seek Camelot?

   _____

6. Do people bathe in Bath? How did the city get its name?

   _____

   _____

7. How did the Industrial Revolution change the British landscape?

   _____

   _____

8. England's entrance to the Chunnel is near _____ in Kent. The train journey from London to Paris on Eurostar takes how long?

   _____

9. What is Hadrian's Wall? Where is it?

   _____

   _____

10. What type of traveler would enjoy a visit to the Channel Islands?

_____

_____

11. Edinburgh's Royal Mile connects two important attractions. What are they?

_____

_____

12. Any golfer visiting Scotland would enjoy a visit to the birthplace of golf at _____ .

13. What are Scotland's two principal outer island chains?

_____

_____

14. The rich tradition of Welsh choral music can be found at annual festivals called

_____ .

15. Ferries sail from the port of _____ in Wales to

_____ in Ireland.

16. What is one of Northern Ireland's legendary geographic attractions?

_____

17. The principal airport gateways to the Emerald Isle are _____ and

_____ .

18. The Ring of Kerry circles the _____ Peninsula on Ireland's

_____ coast.

19. Name three of Dublin's many attractions.

_____

_____

_____

20. Name three islands off the west coast of Ireland that offer visitors a taste of rural life.

_____

_____

_____

# Worksheet 9.3: Itinerary Planning

Name                                                                    Date

Two college students would like to visit London during their winter break when low airfares are a tempting incentive. Their budget is limited. What would you suggest they do during their 1-week trip to the city? How can you help them spend their money wisely? What resources did you use to find the information?

# Worksheet 9.4: Answering Questions

_____
Name                                                              Date

**Directions:** How would you respond to travelers who asked the following questions?

1. "I've heard that England is very expensive. Is there any way to cut costs?"

2. "Should we purchase theater tickets before departing for London? Why or why not?"

# Worksheet 9.5: Map Review

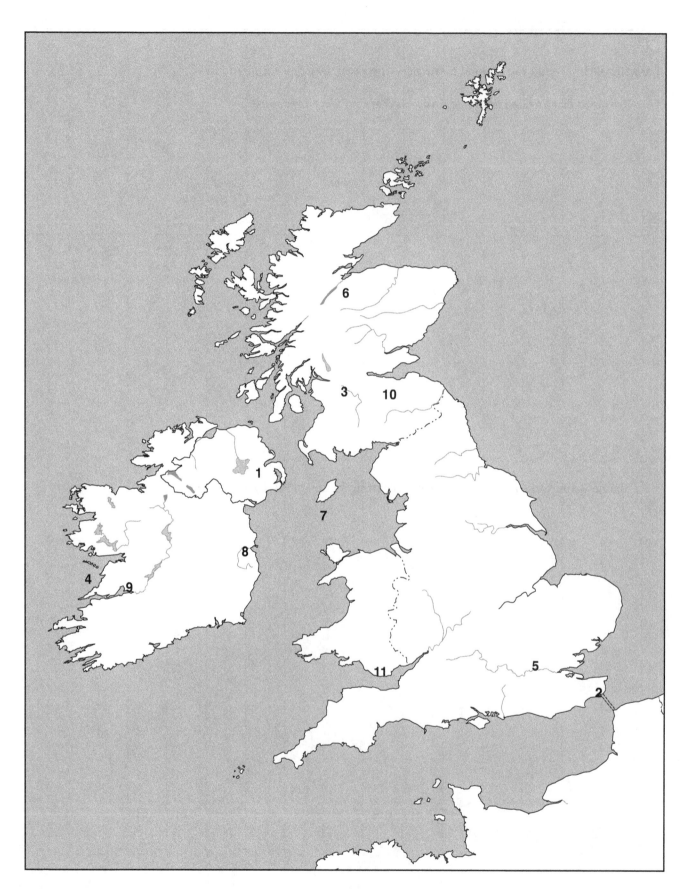

# Worksheet 9.5: Map Review

_____

Name                                                                    Date

**Directions:** Match the destination with its number on the map. Give the three-letter airport code of the destination or of the nearest airport.

**Map Number**                                          **Airport Code**

_____        Aran Islands          _____

_____        Belfast               _____

_____        Cardiff               _____

_____        Dover                 _____

_____        Dublin                _____

_____        Edinburgh             _____

_____        Glasgow               _____

_____        Inverness             _____

_____        Isle of Man           _____

_____        London                _____

_____        Shannon               _____

**Bonus Question:** Name two of the four Channel Islands.

_____

_____

# Worksheet 9.6: Using Reference Materials

Name                                                                    Date

**Directions:** Using available resources, answer the questions in the space provided. Indicate in your answer what resource you used.

1. What documentation does a leisure traveler need to enter Great Britain?

2. What kinds of rail passes are sold for the British Isles?

3. How much are theater tickets to a top London musical?

4. Travelers want to know the dates of the Edinburgh Festival next summer. Can you help them?

5. Are there any special holiday events in London between Christmas and New Year's Day? Are museums and theaters open?

# Worksheet 9.7: Itinerary Planning

---

Name                                                                    Date

The immigrant experience is recent for many Americans, and people of Irish ancestry enjoy going to Ireland to see where their families came from. The Roman Catholic Church has long played a major role in Irish social life. Almost every city has a cathedral with extensive parish records. Plan an 8-day tour for a couple traveling to Ireland to research their roots. Use Web and written resources.

# Worksheet 9.8: Looking Back: A Chapter Quiz

_____
Name                                                                    Date

**Directions:** Answer the questions in the space provided, or circle the correct answer.

1. What is the Commonwealth?

   _____

   _____

2. Is Northern Ireland an independent country?

   _____

3. Name London's three principal airports, and give their three-letter codes.

   _____

   _____

   _____

4. What range of hills is called "the backbone of England"?

   _____

5. England's longest river is the _____ .

6. Ireland's longest river (and the longest river in the British Isles) is the _____ .

7. Which destination is not part of Great Britain?
   A. Scotland
   B. Northern Ireland
   C. Republic of Ireland
   D. Wales

8. The travelers want to see the circle of stones called Stonehenge. To which city would you direct them to find accommodations?
   A. Plymouth
   B. Salisbury
   C. Portsmouth
   D. Southampton

9. What attraction is out of place in this itinerary?
   A. Land's End
   B. York Minster
   C. Poldark tin mine
   D. Tintagel
   E. Jamaica Inn

10. For each statement, circle either True or False.

   True     False     A moor is heavily forested.

   True     False     William the Conqueror was the last foreign invader of England.

   True     False     Westminster Abbey is the burial place of kings and queens, poets, and heroes.

   True     False     Buckingham Palace is the home of England's prime minister.

   True     False     The Thames is the longest river in the British Isles.

   True     False     An *eisteddfod* is a festival of poetry and music.

   True     False     The Chunnel connects England and the Republic of Ireland.

11. Name the capital and principal city of Wales.

   _____

12. The street that connects Edinburgh Castle and the Palace of Holyroodhouse is called
   A. the Royal Mile.
   B. Princes Street.
   C. Argyll Street.
   D. McDouglass Avenue.

13. The Edinburgh International Festival is held each year during the months of

   _____.

14. In Dublin, at Trinity College, visitors can see the famous literary masterpiece, the

   _____.

15. Travelers can kiss the Blarney Stone in southwest Ireland when they visit the city of

   _____.

# CHAPTER 10

# Northern Europe

## ■ Resources

Tourist boards, publications, and industry sources offer a wealth of information about northern Europe. Travelers tend to underestimate distances, traffic, and crowds in Europe. As a result, they often wind up spending more time on the road or waiting around than in actual sightseeing. A tour operator's brochure can help when you are unfamiliar with a destination and need to determine how much distance can be traveled per day.

### Transportation

Auto Europe
www.autoeurope.com

Europcar
www.europcar.com

European rail
www.raileurope.com

River cruises
www.amadeuswaterways.com
www.vikingrivercruises.com

### Austria

www.austria-tourism.com/us

Castle hotels
www.schlosshotels.co.at

Schonbrunn Palace
www.schoenbrunn.at

Vienna
www.wien.info

### Belgium

www.visitbelgium.com

### Denmark

www.visitdenmark.com

Copenhagen
www.visitcopenhagen.dk

### Finland

www.gofinland.org

### Germany

www.cometogermany.com

Castle hotels
www.burghotel.de

### Iceland

www.goiceland.com

Farm holidays
www.farmholidays.is

Reykjavik
www.tourisism.reykjavik.is

### Liechtenstein

(see Switzerland)

**Luxembourg**
www.visitluxembourg.com

**The Netherlands**
www.holland.com

Anne Frank House
www.annefrank.nl

Van Gogh Museum
www.vangoghmuseum.nl

**Norway**
www.visitnorway.com

Coastal voyages
www.hurtigruten.com

**Sweden**
www.visit-sweden.com

Göta Canal
www.gotacanal.com

**Switzerland**
www.myswitzerland.com

Jungfrau Rail
www.jungfraubahn.ch

Lake Geneva
www.lake-geneva-region.ch

Matterhorn
www.matterhornstate.com

Swiss Rail
www.sbb.ch

# ■ UNESCO World Heritage Sites

For northern Europe, the UNESCO World Heritage List includes the following:

## Cultural Heritage

- Aachen (Aix-la-Chapelle) Cathedral, Germany

- Amsterdam, the Netherlands: defense line

- Beemster Polder, the Netherlands

- Belfries of Flanders and Wallonia, Belgium

- Bergen, Norway: Bryggen (wharf)

- Berlin, Germany: museums, including the Pergamon

- Berne, Switzerland: old city

- Bruges, Belgium: historic center

- Brussels, Belgium: Grand-Place

- Cologne Cathedral, Germany

- Dessau and Weimar, Germany: Bauhaus buildings

- Drottingholm Slot (royal palace), Sweden

- Eisleben and Wittenberg, Germany: Luther memorials

- Flemish Béguinages, Belgium

- Graz, Austria: historic center

- Hallstatt-Dachstein-Salzkammergut, Austria: cultural landscape

- Helsinger (Elsinore), Denmark: Kronborg Castle

- Helsinki (Helsingfors), Finland: Suomenlinna Sea Fortress

- Kinderdijk-Elshout, the Netherlands: windmills

- Lübeck, Germany: Hanseatic city

- Luxembourg City, Luxembourg: old town and fortifications
- Salzburg, Austria: historic center, Mozart's birthplace, residence
- Semmering Railway, Austria
- Speyer, Germany: cathedral
- Stockholm, Sweden: Skogskykogarden
- Trier, Germany: Roman monuments
- Urmes stave church, Norway
- Utrecht, the Netherlands
- Vienna, Austria: Schloss Schönbrunn and gardens
- Visby, Sweden: Hanseatic town and Viking site
- Weimar, Germany: classical city
- Würzburg, Germany: Residenz with the court palaces and square

## Natural Heritage

- High Coast, Sweden
- Lapponian area, Sweden
- Messel Pit fossil site, Germany

# ■ Reading Suggestions: Northern Europe

- Hans Christian Andersen (1805–1875): He is internationally known for his fairy tales. Copenhagen's *Little Mermaid* statue is one of the city's most popular attractions.
- Michael Gorra: *The Bells in Their Silence: Travel through Germany* (2004) is a humorous interpretation of modern Germany.
- Christopher Isherwood: *Berlin Stories* (1946) contains stories of social corruption inspired by his life in Germany during Hitler's rise to power and is the basis for the Broadway musical *Cabaret*.
- Stieg Larsson: *The Girl with the Dragon Tattoo* (2008), *The Girl Who Played with Fire* (2009) and *The Girl Who Kicked the Hornet's Nest* (2010) are Swedish crime novels made into films.
- Helen MacInnes: She wrote *The Salzburg Connection* (1963), a thriller.
- Herman Wouk: His novels *The Winds of War* (1971) and *War and Remembrance* (1978), the story of World War II in Europe and the Pacific, were made into a TV mini-series.

# Worksheet 10.1: Geography

_____
Name                                                                    Date

**Directions:** Answer the questions in the space provided.

1. Name the northern European capital that is a major port on the strait connecting the Kattegat with the Baltic Sea.

   _____

2. Active volcanoes, hot springs, and spouting geysers are attractions of _____ .

3. The mountain system dominating the southern part of northern Europe is the _____ .

4. The mountain range that separates Norway and Sweden is _____ .

5. The two peninsulas that dominate northern Europe are the _____ Peninsula

   and the _____ Peninsula.

6. How does the term "Land of the Midnight Sun" affect the traveler?

   _____

7. Describe where the Rhine River flows, from start to finish. What is the most scenic part of the river?

   _____

   _____

   _____

   _____

8. The Danube River flows in a(n) _____ direction to the

   _____ Sea.

9. What causes northern Europe to have a generally milder climate than parts of North America at the same latitude?

   _____

   _____

10. How would you describe the landscape of Finland?

    _____

    _____

11. The _____ Sea separates the European mainland from Great Britain.

12. The _____ Sea separates Sweden from Finland.

# Worksheet 10.2: Itinerary Planning

Name                                                                                    Date

Mr. and Mrs. Schulse are planning a trip to Germany. They want to see King Ludwig's castles, travel the Romantic Road, and perhaps spend a few days at the Oktoberfest. How should you route them? When should they go?

# Worksheet 10.3: Answering Questions

_____
Name                                                                Date

**Directions:** How would you respond to travelers who asked the following questions?

1. "My wife and I will be celebrating our 25th anniversary in Vienna, Austria. Can you recommend any restaurants—not necessarily pricey—that specialize in Viennese cuisine for an anniversary dinner?"

2. "We went to Alaska last summer. Isn't a trip to Scandinavia much the same?"

3. "I've heard that the Nordic countries can be very expensive. Is this true?"

4. "We'd like to go on a river cruise, but won't it be frustrating floating by interesting towns when we want to stop and explore?"

# Worksheet 10.4: Map Review

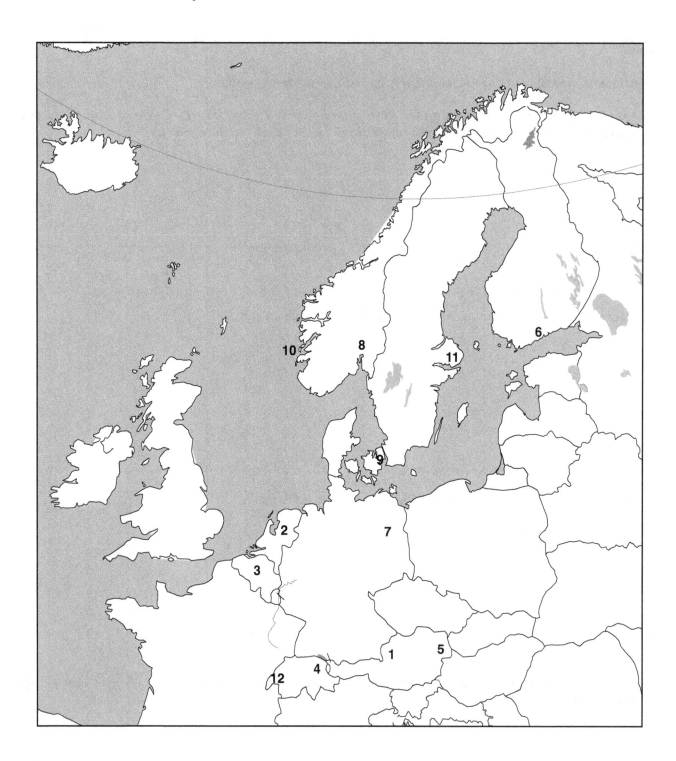

# Worksheet 10.4: Map Review

_____

Name                                                                    Date

**Directions:** Fill in the blanks.

Match the destination with its number on the map. You can use each number only once. Give the three-letter airport code of the destination or of the nearest airport.

**Map Number**                                    **Airport Code**

_____        Amsterdam        _____

_____        Bergen           _____

_____        Berlin           _____

_____        Brussels         _____

_____        Copenhagen       _____

_____        Geneva           _____

_____        Helsinki         _____

_____        Oslo             _____

_____        Salzburg         _____

_____        Stockholm        _____

_____        Vienna           _____

_____        Zürich           _____


**Bonus Question:** Northern Europe is located in the _____ and the

_____ Hemispheres.

# Worksheet 10.5: Using Reference Materials

Name _____ Date _____

**Directions:** Using available resources, answer the questions in the space provided. Indicate in your answer what resource you used.

1. The travelers have taken many trips to Europe but have never been to Belgium or Luxembourg. They are inquiring about train service. How long does it take by train from Paris to Brussels and from Luxembourg City back to Paris?

2. What documentation does the leisure traveler need to enter Finland?

3. The travelers would like tickets to next year's Salzburg Festival. What can you find out about availability and price?

4. What are the embarkation points and attractions of Rhine River cruises? What is the price of an average cabin per person, double occupancy?

# Worksheet 10.6: Looking Back: A Chapter Quiz

Name _____ Date _____

**Directions:** Answer the questions in the space provided, or circle the correct answer.

1. What is the European Union?

   _____

   _____

2. Match the country with its capital. Add the city's three-letter airport code.

| Capital | Capital's Airport Code | Country | |
|---|---|---|---|
| _____ | _____ | Belgium | A. Berlin |
| _____ | _____ | Denmark | B. Oslo |
| _____ | _____ | Finland | C. Stockholm |
| _____ | _____ | Germany | D. Luxembourg |
| _____ | _____ | Iceland | E. Berne |
| _____ | _____ | Liechtenstein | F. Amsterdam |
| _____ | _____ | Luxembourg | G. Brussels |
| _____ | _____ | The Netherlands | H. Helsinki |
| _____ | _____ | Norway | I. Copenhagen |
| _____ | _____ | Sweden | J. Reykjavik |
| _____ | _____ | Switzerland | K. Vaduz |

3. What are the two cultural groups that make up Belgium?

   _____

   _____

4. Travelers wanting to see Norway's fjord coast while traveling on board a coastal steamer should head to the embarkation city of
   A. Oslo.
   B. Trondheim.
   C. Tromsø.
   D. Bergen.

5. Copenhagen's best-known small landmark is the
   A. Lur Blowers.
   B. Little Mermaid.
   C. Radhuspladsen.
   D. Sailor's Memorial.

6. The best clothing advice to give a summer traveler to northern Europe is to bring
   A. jogging clothes.
   B. for men, a suit with a tie; for women, a skirt and blouse.
   C. comfortable shoes, layered clothing, and an umbrella.
   D. shorts and sleeveless tops.

7. The capital city of the European Union is
   A. Amsterdam.
   B. Brussels.
   C. Berlin.
   D. Zürich.

8. To see alpine scenery such as filmed in *The Sound of Music*, travelers should visit Austria and the city of
   A. Salzburg.
   B. Vienna.
   C. Innsbrück.
   D. Kitzbühel.

9. The most scenic part of a Rhine River cruise is between
   A. Mainz and Cologne.
   B. Heidelberg and Frankfurt.
   C. Baden-Baden and Heidelberg.
   D. Bonn and Cologne.

10. One of Brussels's famous attractions is the beautiful medieval square called the
    A. Casemates.
    B. Lower City.
    C. Grand' Place.
    D. Centrum.

11. Travelers wanting to see Holland's polders, windmills, people wearing wooden shoes, and cheese markets should head to
    A. Haarlem and Lisse.
    B. Volendam and Alkmaar.
    C. Scheveningen.
    D. Delft and The Hague.

12. The fairy-tale castles of King Ludwig II are found in which part of Germany?
    A. southeastern
    B. northeastern
    C. southwestern
    D. northwestern

# CHAPTER 11

# Eastern Europe

## ◼ Resources

Tour operators who deal with Eastern Europe on a daily basis are usually good sources of logistical information if you are making a booking with their organization. For other help, turn to the tourist boards.

### Transportation
European rail
www.raileurope.com

### Belarus
www.belarusembassy.com

### Bulgaria
www.bulgariatravel.org

### Czech Republic
www.czechtourism.com

Prague
www.pis.cz

### Estonia
www.visitestonia.com

Tallinn
www.tourism.tallinn.ee

### Hungary
www.gotohungary.com

### Latvia
www.latvia-usa.org

### Lithuania
www.tourismlithuania.org

### Moldova
www.moldova.org

### Poland
www.polandtourism.org

### Romania
www.romaniatourism.com

### Russia
www.russia-travel.com

### Slovakia
www.slovakiatourism.sk

### Slovenia
www.sloveniatravel.com

### Ukraine
www.ukraineinfo.us

# ■ UNESCO World Heritage Sites

For Eastern Europe, the UNESCO World Heritage List includes the following:

## Cultural Heritage

- Auschwitz-Birkenau concentration camp, Poland
- Budapest, Hungary: banks of the Danube and Buda Castle
- Cesky Krumlov, Czech Republic: historic center
- Coronian Spit, Lithuania
- Ferapontov Monastery, Russia
- Holasovice historic village reservation, Czech Republic
- Hollokö, Slovak Republic: traditional village
- Ivanova, Bulgaria: rock chapels
- Kazan Kremlin: Russia
- Kazanluk: Thracian tomb, Bulgaria
- Khizi Pogost, Russia
- Kiev, Ukraine, St. Sophia Cathedral and Lavra of Kyiv-Pechersk
- Kraków historic center, Poland
- Malbork, Poland: Teutonic castle
- Maramures, Romania: wooden churches
- Mir, Belarus: castle complex
- Moldavian churches, Romania
- Moscow, Russia: Church of the Ascension at Kolomenskoye
- Moscow, Russia: Kremlin, Red Square, and St. Basil's Cathedral
- Novgorod, Russia: historic monuments and surroundings
- Prague, Czech Republic: historic center
- Riga, Latvia: historic center
- Rila, Bulgaria: monastery
- St. Petersburg, Russia: historic center with Hermitage Museum
- Sighisoara, Romania: historic center
- Solovetskiye Ostrova cultural and historic area, Russia
- St. Petersburg, Russia: historic center with Hermitage Museum
- Sveshtari, Bulgaria: Thracian tomb
- Tallinn, Estonia: historic center
- Vilnius, Lithuania: old city
- Vlkolinec, Slovak Republic
- Warsaw, Poland: historic center
- Wieliczka, Poland: salt mines

## Natural Heritage

- Aggtalek Caves and the Slovak karst, Hungary/Slovak Republic

- Bialowieza Forest, Poland/Belarus

- Danube Delta, Romania

- Golden Mountains of Altay, Russia

- Kamchatka volcanoes, Russia

- Komi virgin forests, Russia

- Lake Baikal, Russia

- Pirin National Park, Bulgaria

- *Srebarna Nature Reserve, Bulgaria

- Western Caucasus, Russia

# ■ Reading Suggestions: Eastern Europe

Travelers to Eastern Europe benefit from background reading. Much of the history and many of the sites are unknown to the typical tourist.

- Anne Applebaum: *Gulag: A History* (2004) tells of the origins and evolution of the notorious labor camps in post-revolutionary Russia.

- Stephanie Elizondo Griest: *Around the Bloc: My Life in Moscow, Beijing, and Havana* (2004) recounts a university student's year abroad in Moscow and gives a tour of what's left of the communist bloc.

- Robert K. Massie: *Nicholas and Alexandra* (1967) is a story of the last tsar and his family.

- James Michener: *Poland* (1983) blends history and fiction.

- Simon Sebag Montefiore: *Stalin: The Court of the Red Tsar* (2004) provides a portrait of the dictator fashioned from newly opened archives.

- Boris Pasternak: *Doctor Zhivago* (1957) won a Nobel Prize, which Pasternak had to reject because of the furor the novel triggered in the Soviet Union.

- Edward Rutherfurd: Like Michener, Rutherfurd makes his fictional characters take second place to historical events in *Russka* (1991).

- Alexander Solzhenitsyn: *The Gulag Archipelago* (1973) details the terror of Stalin's reign.

- Bram Stoker: *Dracula* (1897) is a novel about vampires in Transylvania and England.

# Worksheet 11.1: Geography

_____     _____
Name                                                                          Date

**Directions:** Answer the questions in the space provided.

1. What is Eastern Europe's dominant geographic feature?

_____

2. Name the Baltic States. Why do they have that name?

_____

_____

_____

3. Where does Asia start and Europe end?

_____

_____

4. What are the steppes? Where in Eastern Europe are they found?

_____

_____

5. Europe's longest river, the Volga, begins southeast of _____

and flows south to the _____ Sea.

6. Where was the world's worst nuclear disaster?

_____

7. What sort of weather should the traveler expect when visiting Moscow in the summer?

_____

8. Which Baltic country is closest to Finland and is often visited on 1-day tours from Helsinki?

_____

9. What natural resource has attracted tourists to the Czech cities of Carlsbad and Marienbad for centuries?

_____

10. Most of eastern Hungary is an area of great plains called the _____ .

11. Eastern Russia is the site of the world's deepest lake, Lake _____ .

12. Name three Eastern European countries bordering the Black Sea.

_____

_____

_____

# Worksheet 11.2: Itinerary Planning

Name _____  Date _____

Mr. and Mrs. Vaclav Lepescu request your help. They plan to fly into Munich, want to rent a car there and drive to Prague, and then plan to visit Vienna before heading back to Munich. Mr. Lepescu says: "I've heard that driving into the Czech Republic may be difficult and expensive, but we enjoy the freedom of stopping along the way and doing our own thing." What can you find out about auto rental in the area? How would you route the couple?

# Worksheet 11.3: Answering Questions

_____
Name                                                          Date

**Directions:** How would you respond to travelers who asked the following questions?

1. "How do most people travel across Russia? Is it possible to drive?"

2. "I've heard the hotels in Russia are like barracks. Is that true?"

3. "We want to explore on our own and try the Moscow Metro, but we don't know how to deal with the unfamiliar alphabet. What can we do?"

# Worksheet 11.4: Map Review

# Worksheet 11.4 Map Review

_____

Name                                                                    Date

**Directions:** Match the destination with its number on the map. Give the three-letter airport code of the destination or of the nearest airport.

**Map Number**                          **Airport Code**

_____        Bratislava       _____

_____        Bucharest        _____

_____        Budapest         _____

_____        Kiev             _____

_____        Minsk            _____

_____        Moscow           _____

_____        Prague           _____

_____        Riga             _____

_____        St. Petersburg   _____

_____        Sofia            _____

_____        Tallinn          _____

_____        Vilnius          _____

_____        Warsaw           _____

**Bonus Question:** It is 1700 standard time in your hometown. What time is it in Moscow?

_____

# Worksheet 11.5: Using Reference Materials

_____

Name                                                    Date

**Directions:** Using available resources, answer the questions in the space provided. Indicate in your answer what resource you used.

The travelers are planning an independent trip in July to visit relatives in Moscow.

1. How would you route them by air from your home to their destination?

2. What documentation do they need?

3. Are there any health concerns? If so, what are they?

4. Their relatives' apartment is too small for guests. Where would they stay in Moscow?

5. Do you have any suggestions for sightseeing? They would like to see the Bolshoi Ballet. Is this possible?

# Worksheet 11.6: Looking Back: A Chapter Quiz

_____

Name                                                                    Date

**Directions:** Answer the following questions.

1. Match the Eastern European attraction with its city.

   _____        Budapest          A. Kremlin

   _____        Czestochowa       B. Hermitage Museum

   _____        Kraków            C. Song festivals

   _____        Moscow            D. Royal Palace on Wawel Hill

   _____        Prague            E. Black Madonna

   _____        St. Petersburg    F. Wilanow Palace

   _____        Tallinn           G. Charles Bridge

   _____        Warsaw            H. Fishermen's Bastion

2. Mark each statement True or False.

   True      False      European spas offer health treatments.

   True      False      Lithuania is the most developed of the Baltic States.

   True      False      Russian people are all of the same ethnic background.

   True      False      The Czech Republic is ready for tourism.

   True      False      Moscow's winters are mild and its summers cold.

   True      False      The Danube Bend is between Esztergom and Visegrád.

   True      False      Eastern cuisine is heavy on salads and light on meat and potatoes.

   True      False      GUM on Red Square is a large department store.

   True      False      St. Petersburg is Russia's second-largest city, with famous museums and palaces.

# CHAPTER 12

# Southern Europe

## ◼ Resources

### Transportation

European rail
www.raileurope.com

### Albania

www.albaniantourism.com

### Andorra

www.turisme.ad

### Bosnia-Herzegovina

www.mvp.gov.ba

### Croatia

www.croatia.hr

### Cyprus

www.visitcyprus.org

### France

www.franceguide.com

Balloon trips
www.bombardsociety.com

Chenonceaux
www.chenonceau.com

Corsica
www.visit-corsica.com

### Macedonia

None

Eiffel Tower
www.tour-eiffel.fr

French Country Waterways
www.fcwl.com

Gites de France
www.gites-de-france.fr

Louvre
www.louvre.fr

Paris
www.paris-touristoffice.com

Versailles
www.chateauversailles.fr

### Gibraltar

www.gibraltar.gov.gil

### Greece

www.gnto.gr

### Italy

www.italiantourism.com

Farmhouse rentals
www.agriturist.it

Spas
www.spas.it

Trains
www.trenitalia.com

Villas
www.italianvillas.com

## Malta
www.visitmalta.co

## Monaco
www.visitmonaco.com

## Portugal
www.portugal.org

Gulbenkian
www.museu.gulbenkian.pt

Pousadas
www.pousadas.pt

## Serbia and Montenegro
www.belgradetourism.org.yu

## Spain
www.okspain.org

Guggenheim Bilbao
www.guggenheim-bilbao.es

La Sagrada Familia
www.sagradafamilia.org

Paradors
www.parador.es

## Vatican City
www.vatican.va (Press Office)

## Yugoslavia
www.belgradetourism.org.yu

# ■ UNESCO World Heritage Sites

For southern Europe, the UNESCO World Heritage List includes the following:

## Cultural Heritage

- Agrigento, Sicily, Italy: archaeological area
- Alberobello, Italy: Trulli houses
- Altamira, Spain: caves and archaeological site
- Amalfi Coast, Italy
- Assisi, Italy: sites associated with St. Frances
- Athens, Greece: Acropolis
- Avignon, France: Palace of the Popes
- Barcelona, Spain: Parque and Palacio Güell and Casa Milá
- Canal du Midi, France
- Carcassonne, France: historic fortified city
- Chambord, France: chateaux and estate
- Chartres, France: cathedral
- Cinque Terre, Italy: Portovénere
- Córdoba, Spain: mosque and historic center
- Delphi, Greece: archaeological site
- Dubrovnik, Croatia: old city
- El Escorial, Spain: palace and monastery
- Epidaurus, Greece: archaeological site
- Évora, Portugal: historic center
- Florence, Italy: historic center, Duomo, Uffizi, and Ponte Vecchio

- Fontainebleau, France: palace and park
- Granada, Spain: Alhambra, Generalife, and Albaicín quarter
- Hadrian's Villa, Italy
- Vallée du Vézère, France: Lascaux and other grottoes
- Loire Valley, between Chalonnes and Sully-sur-Loire, France
- Malta, Ggantija: megalithic temples
- Météora, Greece: rock monasteries
- Milan, Italy: *The Last Supper*
- Mont-St-Michel and its bay, France
- Naples, Italy: historic center
- Olympia, Greece: archaeological site
- Paris, France: banks of the Seine, Eiffel Tower, Louvre, Musée d'Orsay, and Notre-Dame
- Pisa, Italy: Piazza del Duomo and Leaning Tower
- Pompeii, Herculaneum, and Torre Annunziata, Italy: archaeological areas
- Porto (Oporto), Portugal: historic center
- Ravenna, Italy: early Christian monuments and mosaics
- Reims, France: Cathedral Notre-Dame
- Rhodes, Greece: medieval city
- Rome, Italy: historic center
- San Gimignano, Italy: historic center and towers
- Sardinia, Italy: Su Nuraxi di Barúmini
- Segovia, Spain: old town and aqueduct
- Seville, Spain: cathedral, Alcazar, and Archivo de Indias
- Siena, Italy: historic center, Piazza del Campo
- Sintra, Portugal: historic city
- Split, Croatia: historic center with Diocletian palace
- Tarragona, Spain Roman city
- Toledo, Spain: historic city
- Valletta, Malta: old city
- Vatican City, Italy
- Venice, Italy: lagoon and Basilica di San Marco
- Verona, Italy: historic city
- Versailles, France: palace and park
- Vicenza, Italy: city and Palladian villas of the Veneto
- Way of St. James pilgrimage route (Camino de Santiago) through France and Spain

## Natural Heritage

- Athens, Greece

- Banks of the Seine: Paris, France

- Durmitor National Park, Serbia and Montenegro

- Golfe de Girolate and Reserve Naturelle, Corsica, France

- Ibiza, Spain: biodiversity and culture

- Ísole Eólie (Lipari), Italy

- *Kotor and its gulf, Serbia and Montenegro

- Laurisilva of Madeira, Portugal

- Metéora, Greece

- Mont Perdu/Monte Pedido, France/Spain

- Mont-Saint-Michel and its bay, France

- Ohrid Lake region, Macedonia

- Parque Nacional coto de Doñana, Spain

- Parque Nacional de Garajonay, Gomera, Canary Islands, Spain

- Plitvice Lakes National Park, Croatia

- Skocjan Caves, Slovenia

# ■ Reading Suggestions: Southern Europe

- Carol Drinkwater: *Olive Season* (2003) is a romance set in Provence, France.

- Lawrence Durrell (1912–1990): His fiction and non-fiction books are about the Mediterranean and Aegean islands, where Durrell lived and worked for many years for the British Foreign Office.

- Umberto Eco: *The Name of the Rose* (1980) is a medieval mystery.

- E. M. Forster: *A Room with a View* (1961) is a novel about Florence and the English.

- Robert Harris: *Pompeii* (2004) is a novel to read before, while, or instead of traveling to the ruins.

- Ernest Hemingway: *For Whom the Bell Tolls* (1940) is a novel based on the author's experiences in Spain during the Spanish Civil War.

- Washington Irving: *Legends of the Alhambra* (1832–1852) is a story about the clashes between the Spaniards and the Moors, written while Irving was an attaché at the American legation in Madrid.

- Nikos Kazantzakis: *Zorba the Greek* (1946) is a novel that was turned into a film and Broadway musical.

- Frances Mayes: *Under the Tuscan Sun* (1996) is a memoir of a house restoration in Tuscany.

- Peter Mayle: *A Year in Provence* and *Toujours Provence* (1971) are about an English couple building a house in the south of France. *A Good Year* (2004) is also about France.

- James Michener: *The Drifters* (1971) is a novel about six runaways adrift in Spain, Marrakesh, and Mozambique.

- Daphne Phelps: In *A House in Sicily* (1999), the author falls in love with a house, a community, and a way of life.

- Sidney Sheldon: *Other Side of Midnight* (1973), a story of tycoons, Paris, D.C., and a villa on a Greek island, was a best-seller and eventually a movie.

- Patrick Süskind: *Perfume* (1986) is a medieval detective story about the "nose" needed for perfume development.

- Emma Tennant: *A House in Corfu* (2002) details the delights and frustrations of a family's daily life on a Greek island.

# Worksheet 12.1: Geography

Name _____  Date _____

**Directions:** Answer the questions in the space provided.

1. What do people mean when they say a destination has a "Mediterranean climate"?

   _____

   _____

2. Southern Europe has three large peninsulas. Name them.

   _____

   _____

   _____

3. What is the name of the strait that connects the Mediterranean Sea and the Atlantic Ocean?

   _____

4. Portugal's and Spain's southern coasts are well known to vacationers. In Portugal, this coastal area is the

   _____.

   In Spain, the region is called the

   _____.

5. Which Mediterranean island is the most easterly?

   _____

   Which island is the largest?

   _____

   Which ones belong to Spain?

   _____

   Which one belongs to France?

   _____

6. Name the mountain range that separates Spain from France.

   _____

7. The mountains that form the spine of Italy are the

_____.

8. The Balkan Peninsula extends out from the European mainland in the east. As many as ten countries can be considered part of the Balkans. Name at least seven.

_____

_____

_____

_____

_____

_____

9. The river running through the heart of Paris is the Seine, but the French river most famous for its châteaux, castles, and scenery is the

_____.

10. The Isthmus of Corinth connects mainland Greece to the _____ Peninsula.

11. Why is Cyprus divided?

_____

_____

12. Where is the Rock of Gibraltar? Which country controls it? Which country wants it?

_____

_____

_____

# Worksheet 12.2: Itinerary Planning

Name                                                                        Date

Salvatore de Trevi wants a bike trip through Italy. He is willing to consider a tour group, but hopefully one that caters to young single travelers. Do you have any suggestions as to region and routing?

# Worksheet 12.3: Answering Questions

_____

Name                                                                    Date

**Directions:** How would you respond to travelers who asked the following questions?

1. "I'm planning a trip to Greece. Would travel insurance cover a cancellation in case of a U.S. State Department recommendation against nonessential travel or a terrorist attack there?"

2. "I want to see the Sistine Chapel, but is there any way to avoid the crowds?"

# Worksheet 12.4: Map Review

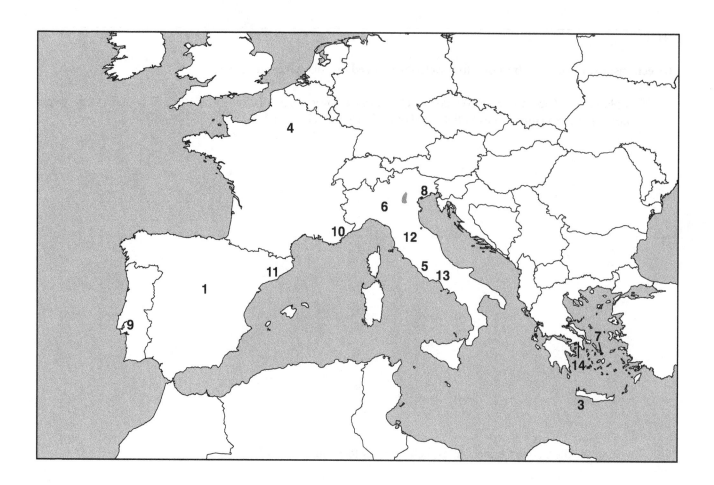

# Worksheet 12.4: Map Review

_____
Name                                                                    Date

**Directions:** Match the destination with its corresponding number on the map. Give the three-letter airport code of the destination or of the nearest airport.

**Map Number**                                    **Airport Code**

_____        Athens          _____

_____        Barcelona       _____

_____        Crete           _____

_____        Cyprus          _____

_____        Florence        _____

_____        Lisbon          _____

_____        Madrid          _____

_____        Milan           _____

_____        Mykonos         _____

_____        Naples          _____

_____        Nice            _____

_____        Paris           _____

_____        Rome            _____

_____        Venice          _____

**Bonus Question:** How many time zones are there in southern Europe?

_____

# Worksheet 12.5: Using Reference Materials

Name                                                                    Date

**Directions:** Using available resources, answer the questions in the space provided. Indicate in your answer what resource you used.

1. The travelers are planning an independent trip to France in the spring. How would you route them by air from your city?

2. What documentation do they need to enter France?

3. They have a limited budget. Where could they stay in Paris?

4. What suggestions do you have for 3 days of city sightseeing?

# Worksheet 12.6: Looking Back: A Chapter Quiz

_____
Name                                                                    Date

**Directions:** Answer the questions in the space provided, or circle the correct answer.

1. The two small independent countries within Italy are _____

   and _____ .

2. Match each description with its museum by writing the letter of the correct description in the blank.

   _____ Uffizi          A. Museum in Paris, the largest in the world

   _____ Vatican         B. Museum in Madrid with works by Spanish masters

   _____ Prado           C. Museum with the world's largest religious collection

   _____ Louvre          D. Museum with the art collection of the Medici family

3. The World War II D-Day beaches are found in the French province of _____ .

4. Europe's largest medieval fortress can be explored at _____ .

5. Accommodations in Spain include the _____ , a network of state-owned and -operated hotels.

6. One of Barcelona's favorite sons is architect
   A. Jose Sert.
   B. Andrés Segovia.
   C. Antoni Gaudí.
   D. Miguel de Cervantes.

7. The Alhambra is found in _____ .

8. The so-called capital of the Algarve and the site of its airport is _____ .

9. Name the southern European country whose heads of state are the president of France and the bishop of Urgell.

   _____

10. Italy's largest lake is _____ .

11. The oldest quarter of Athens, with restaurants and bars providing activity until late at night, is called the

    _____ .

12. For each statement, circle True or False.

    True     False     Landmarks in Rome include the Doge's Palace, St. Mark's Square, and the Murano glass-working center.

    True     False     Southern Greece consists of the flat Peloponnese Peninsula.

| True | False | The Mediterranean cruise season begins around Easter and continues until early October. |
| True | False | Piraeus is the port of Athens. |
| True | False | Rhodes is the largest of the Greek islands. |

# CHAPTER 13

# Africa and the Middle East

## ■ Resources

**Botswana**
www.govbw/tourism

**Egypt**
www.touregypt.net

**Israel**
www.goisrael.com

**Morocco**
www.tourisme-marocain.com

**Namibia**
www.namibiatourism.co.uk

**South Africa**
www.southafrica.net

Blue Train
www.bluetrain.co.za

Cape Town
www.cape-town.org

Rovos Rail
www.rovos.co.za

**Tanzania**
www.tanzania tourism.org

**Turkey**
www.tourismturkey.org

**Zambia**
www.zambiatourism.com

Zambezi Swing
www.thezambeziswing.com

**Zimbabwe**
www.zimbabwetourism.co.zw

## ■ UNESCO World Heritage Sites

For Africa and the Middle East, the UNESCO World Heritage List includes the following:

### Cultural Heritage

- ■ *Abomey, Benin: royal palaces
- ■ Abu Simbel to Philae, Egypt: Nubian monuments
- ■ Accra and Volta, Ghana: forts and castles

- Algiers, Algeria: casbah
- Baalbek, Lebanon
- *Bahia, Oman: fort
- Baku, Azerbaijan: walled city
- Cairo, Egypt: Egyptian Museum
- Carthage, Tunisia: archaeological site
- Damascus, Syria: ancient city
- Fèz, Morocco: medina
- Frankincense Trail, Oman
- Great Zimbabwe National Monument, Zimbabwe
- Halab, Syria: ancient city of Aleppo
- Ile de Gorée, Senegal
- Isfahan, Iran: Meidam Emam
- *Jerusalem, Israel: old city and walls
- Khami Ruins National Monument, Zimbabwe
- Lalibela, Ethiopia: rock-hewn churches
- Marrakesh, Morocco: medina
- Meknès, Morocco: historic city
- Memphis, Egypt: pyramid fields from Giza to Dashur
- Persepolis, Iran: ancient city
- Petra, Jordan
- Robben Island, South Africa
- San'a, Yemen: old city
- Sterkfontein and environs, South Africa: fossil hominid sites
- Sukar, Nigeria: cultural landscape
- Tadrart Acacus, Libya: rock art sites
- Thebes, Egypt: ancient city and necropolis
- *Timbuktu, Mali
- uKhahlamba-Drakensberg Park, South Africa
- Zanzibar, Tanzania: stone town

## Natural Heritage

- *Air and Ténéré Natural Reserves, Niger
- Arabian Oryx Sanctuary, Oman
- Banc d'Arguin National Park, Mauritania
- Bandiagara cliffs, Land of the Dogun, Mali
- Bwindi Impenetrable Forest, Uganda
- *Djoudj National Bird Sanctuary, Senegal
- Gough Island Wildlife Reserve, South Atlantic Ocean, west of African continent

- Greater St. Lucia Wetland Park, South Africa
- Groupe d'Aldabra, Seychelles
- Ichkeul National Park, Tunisia
- Kilimanjaro National Park, Tanzania
- Lake Malawi National Park, Malawi
- Mana Pools National Park and Sapi and Chewore safari areas, Zimbabwe
- Mount Kenya National Park and forest, Kenya
- *Mount Nimba Nature Reserve, Guinea/Côte d'Ivorie
- Ngorongoro Conservation Area, Tanzania
- *Parc National de la Garamba, Congo-Kinshasa
- Parc National de la Komoé, Côte d'Ivorie
- *Parc National de la Salonga, Congo-Kinshasa
- *Parc National de Manova-Gounda-St. Floris, Central African Republic
- Parc National de Tai, Côte d'Ivorie
- *Parc National des Virunga, Congo-Kinshasa
- *Parc National du Kahuzi-Biega, Congo-Kinshasa
- Parc National du Niololo Koba, Senegal
- Parc National du "W," Niger
- Réserve du Dja, Cameroon
- *Réserve du Okapi, Congo-Kinshasa
- Réserve du Tsingy Bemaraha, Madagascar
- *Ruwenzori Mountains National Park, Uganda
- Selous Game Reserve, Tanzania
- Serengeti National Park, Tanzania
- Sibiloe and Central Island National Parks, Kenya
- *Simien National Park, Ethiopia
- Tassili n'Ajjer, Algeria
- uKhahlamba-Drakensberg Park, South Africa
- Vallée de Mai Nature Reserve, Seychelles
- Victoria Falls, Zambia/Zimbabwe

# ■ Reading Suggestions: Africa and the Middle East

- Bartle Bull: *Café on the Nile* (1998) offers romance and adventure in East Africa.
- Sir Richard Francis Burton: This English explorer wrote travel books, including *First Footsteps in Eastern Africa* (1856), an account of his discovery of Lake Tanganyika.

- James Chavell: *Whirlwind* (1986) is a novel set against the 1979 revolution in Iran.

- Agatha Christie: She wrote *Murder on the Orient Express* (1934), which was filmed several times.

- Isak Dinesen (Karen Blixen): *Out of Africa* (1937) begins, "I had a farm in Africa, at the foot of the Ngong Hills"; the renowned work was also filmed.

- Sean Fraser: *African Adventure Atlas* (2004) is a *National Geographic* wish book of route maps that suggest adventure activities in Africa.

- Nadine Gordimer: She is a South African novelist, short story writer, and winner of the Nobel Prize for literature in 1991.

- Ernest Hemingway: *The Short, Happy Life of Francis Macomber* (1938) is a short story of an American couple on safari in Africa.

- James Michener: *The Covenant* (1980) provides a history of South Africa.

- Elizabeth Peters: *The Snake, the Crocodile, and the Dog* (1992) and *Night Train to Memphis* (1994) are detective stories set amidst Egyptian ruins.

- Robert Ruark: *Something of Value* (1955) is an out-of-print novel (available through libraries) of Kenya, safaris, and the Mau Mau uprisings.

- Alexander McCall Smith: *The No. 1 Ladies Detective Agency* (1996) is a best-selling series with descriptions of Botswana's landscape, people, and lifestyles.

- Paul Theroux: *Dark Star Safari* (2003) describes an overland journey from Cairo to Cape Town.

- Leon Uris: *Exodus* (1958) is a classic best-seller about the birth of Israel.

# Worksheet 13.1: Geography

_____
Name                                                                    Date

**Directions:** Answer the questions in the space provided.

1. Which country—home to 125 tribal groups, Ngorongoro Crater, Mount Kilimanjaro, Olduvai Gorge, and Serengeti National Park—is the largest in East Africa?

   _____

2. Africa is linked to the Middle East by the _____ Peninsula.

3. The _____ Gulf separates the Arabian Peninsula from Iran.

4. Describe the Sahel. Why is the region shrinking?

   _____

   _____

   _____

5. Africa's tallest mountain is _____ .

6. Africa's tallest mountains rise near the equator. Given their location, how do you explain the fact that the mountains have glaciers and are snow-covered much of the year?

   _____

   _____

7. The river system that begins in the mountains of Turkey and flows south through Syria and Iraq is the

   _____ .

8. Describe the climate of South Africa.

   _____

   _____

9. Africa has the world's largest desert and the world's longest river. What are they?

   _____

10. When would be the most ideal time to take a safari? Why?

   _____

   _____

11. Which African country produces the most gold?

_____

12. Africa's largest lake is _____ .

13. Where is the Barbary Coast?

_____

14. The country that lies completely within South Africa is _____ .

# Worksheet 13.2: Itinerary Planning

---

Name                                                                    Date

A trip to Egypt is usually a once-in-a-lifetime event. How would you plan a 2-week vacation for Mr. and Mrs. Steven Jones? They have traveled extensively throughout the United States and Europe but have never ventured to an exotic destination. What do they need to know? What attractions are must-sees? When should they go?

# Worksheet 13.3: Answering Questions

_____
Name                                                          Date

**Directions:** How would you respond to travelers who asked the following questions?

1. "Are there any cruise itineraries that include ports along the North African coast of the Mediterranean as well as European ports?"

2. "I'm not very good at bargaining, and I understand that to buy anything in Morocco, I must at least attempt to haggle. What should I do?"

# Worksheet 13.4: Map Review

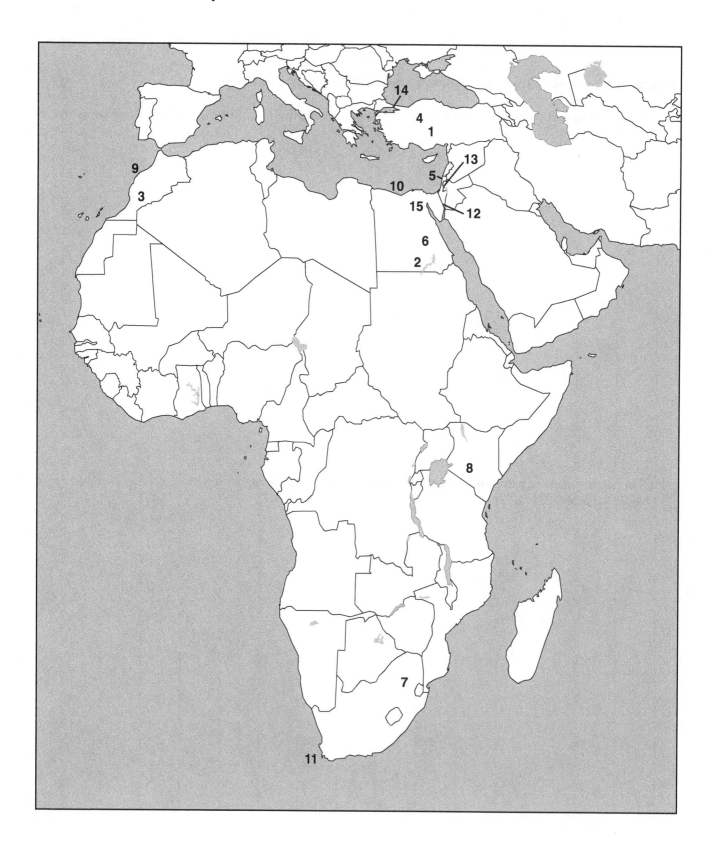

# Worksheet 13.4: Map Review

| Name | Date |
|---|---|

**Directions:** Match the destination with its number on the map. Give the three-letter airport code of the destination or of the nearest airport.

**Map Number**                                   **Airport Code**

_____         Abu Simbel          _____

_____         Alexandria          _____

_____         Ankara              _____

_____         Cairo               _____

_____         Cape Town           _____

_____         Cappadocia          _____

_____         Casablanca          _____

_____         Eilat               _____

_____         Istanbul            _____

_____         Jerusalem           _____

_____         Johannesburg        _____

_____         Luxor               _____

_____         Marrakesh           _____

_____         Nairobi             _____

_____         Tel Aviv            _____

**Bonus Question:** If you find yourself at zero degrees latitude and zero degrees longitude, where are you?

# Worksheet 13.5: Using Reference Materials

| | |
|---|---|
| Name | Date |

**Directions:** Using available resources, answer the questions in the space provided. Indicate in your answer what resource you used.

1. Does the U.S. State Department have any advisories about travel to African countries? If so, which ones?

2. What documentation does a U.S. traveler need to visit Tanzania?

3. Does Tanzania have any health problems travelers should be aware of?

4. What is the weather like in Tanzania in March?

# Worksheet 13.6: Looking Back: A Chapter Quiz

_____
Name                                                              Date

**Directions:** Answer the questions in the space provided, or circle the correct answer.

1. Where are Egypt's most famous pyramids located?

   _____

2. Which African country owes some of its popularity to a series of best-selling detective novels set in this politically stable and geographically unique destination?

   _____

3. How many religions have holy sites in Jerusalem? Name these religions.

   _____

   _____

   _____

   _____

4. Match these Moroccan place-names with their descriptions.

   _____ Casablanca       A. Site of a great square and the place to see snake charmers, visit fortune-tellers, and buy some false teeth

   _____ Rabat            B. Capital and second largest city of Morocco

   _____ Meknes           C. Largest city and the country's international gateway

   _____ Fez              D. City on the north coast across from Spain that receives many day-trippers

   _____ Marrakesh        E. Site of the great medina and Bâb el-Mansour

   _____ Tangier          F. Site of the Karaouine Mosque and one of Islam's oldest universities

5. Match these Egyptian place-names with their descriptions.

   _____ Aswan            A. Temple that was raised to higher ground to save it from the rising waters of the Nile during the construction of the Aswan high dam

   _____ Luxor            B. Africa's largest city

   _____ Abu Simbel       C. Location across the Nile from the Valley of the Kings

   _____ Cairo            D. Popular winter resort

6. **Directions:** Indicate whether each statement is True or False.

| | | |
|---|---|---|
| True | False | A week would be an ample amount of time for a safari. |
| True | False | Thirty to forty people is a good number for an enjoyable safari. |
| True | False | The pyramids at Giza are one of the Seven Wonders of the ancient world. |
| True | False | The Muslim workweek is from sunrise on Saturday through sunset on Thursday. |
| True | False | Light clothing is all that is needed for any trip to Egypt. |
| True | False | Ben Gurion International Airport in Tel Aviv is Israel's principal international airport. |
| True | False | Visitors are welcome in the mosques of Turkey, although they may not enter certain areas. |
| True | False | Cappadocia is a vast volcanic plateau distinguished by its many strange rock formations. |

# CHAPTER 14

# Asia

## ■ Resources

**Bangladesh**
www.parjatan.org

**Bhutan**
www.tourism.gov.bt

**China**
www.cnto.org

Hong Kong
www.discoverhongkong.com

**India**
www.incredibleindia.org

Indian Rail
www.indianrail.gov.in

Taj hotels
www.tajhotels.com

**Indonesia**
www.goindo.com

**Japan**
www.japanwelcomesyou.com

Ryokan Association
www.ryokan.or.jp

**Korea**
www.tour2korea.com

**Laos**
www.visit-laos.com

**Malaysia**
www.tourismmalaysia.com

**Mongolia**
www.mongoliatourism.gov.mn

**Myanmar**
www.myanmar-tourism.com

**Nepal**
www.welcomenepal.com

**Philippines**
www.wowphilippines.com

**Singapore**
www.tourismsingapore.com

**Taiwan, Republic of China**
www.tbroc.gov.tw

**Thailand**
www.tourismthailand.org

Bangkok
www.bangkok.com

**Vietnam**
www.vn-tourism.com

# ■ UNESCO World Heritage Sites

For Asia, the UNESCO World Heritage List includes the following:

## Cultural Heritage

- Agra Fort, India

- Agra, India: Taj Mahal

- Ajanta Caves, India

- Anaradhapura, Sri Lanka: sacred city

- *Angkor, Cambodia

- Ayutthaya and its region, Thailand: historic towns

- Beijing, China: imperial tombs, palaces, Forbidden City, and Summer Palace

- Borobudur, Java, Indonesia: temple compound

- Dambulla Golden Rock Temple, Sri Lanka

- Darjeeling Himalayan railway, India

- Elephanta Caves, India

- Ellora Temple Caves, India

- Gansu, China: Mogau Caves

- Goa, India: churches and monuments

- Great Wall of China

- Hiroshima, Japan: peace memorial

- Hoe An, Vietnam: ancient town

- Hue, Vietnam: monument complex

- Itsukushima Shrine, Japan

- Kandy, Sri Lanka: Temple of the Sacred Tooth

- Kathmandu Valley, Nepal

- Kyongju, Republic of Korea: historic areas

- Kyoto, Japan: ancient city

- *Lahore, Pakistan: fort and Shalimar gardens

- Lhasa, Tibet, China: Potala Palace and Jokhang Temple Monastery

- Luang Prabang, Laos

- Lumbini, Nepal: birthplace of the Lord Buddha

- Nikko, Japan: shrines and temples

- Prambanan, Java, Indonesia: temple compound

- Qufu, Shandong, China: temple and cemetery of Confucius

- Sangiran, Indonesia: early human site

- Seoul, Republic of Korea: palace complex

- Shirakawa-go and Gokayama, Japan: historic villages
- Sokkuram Grotto and Pulguksa Temple, Republic of Korea
- Sukhothai and its region, Thailand: historic towns
- Xi'an area, China: Terracotta Warriors
- Zhoukoudian, China: archaeological site (Peking Man)

## Natural Heritage

- Dambulla Golden Rock Temple, Sri Lanka
- Emei Shan and Leshan Giant Buddha, Sichuan, China
- Gunung Mulu National Park, Malaysia
- Ha Long Bay, Vietnam
- Huang Shan, Anhui, China
- Huanglong scenic and historic interest area, Sichuan, China
- Jiuzhaigou Valley scenic and historic interest area, Sichuan, China
- Kaziranga National Park, India
- Keoladeo National Park, India
- Komodo National Park, Indonesia
- Lorentz National Park, Indonesia
- *Manas Wildlife Sanctuary, India
- Nanda Devi National Park, India
- Puerto-Princesa Subterranean River, Philippines
- Royal Chitwan National Park, Nepal
- Sagarmatha National Park, Nepal
- Shirakami-Sanchi, Japan
- Sinharaja Forest Reserve, Sri Lanka
- Sukhothai and its region and historic towns, Thailand
- Sundarbans, Bangladesh
- Sundarbans National Park, India
- Tai Shan, Shandong, China
- Thung Yai-Huai Kha Khaeng Wildlife Sanctuaries, Thailand
- Tubbataha Reef Marine Park, Philippines
- Ujung Kulon National Park and Krakatau Nature Reserve, Indonesia
- Wulingyuan scenic and historic interest area, Hunan, China
- Wuyl Shan, Fujian, China
- Yaku-shima, Japan

# ■ Reading Suggestions: Asia

- Pearl Buck: *Imperial Woman* (1956). Another view of the empress. Buck, raised in China, won the Pulitzer Prize in 1932 for *The Good Earth* and the Nobel Prize for literature in 1938.

- Bartle Bull: *Shanghai Station* (2004) is set in 1917 at the start of Chiang Kai-shek's and Mao Tse-tung's fight for the mastery of China.

- James Clavell: *Shogun* (1975) is about Japan in the 1600s. *Tai-Pan* (1966) and *Noble House* (1981), both set in Hong Kong.

- Bruce Feiler: *Learning to Bow* (1991) is a funny book about the culture clash between the United States and Japan.

- Edward M. Forster: *A Passage to India* (1924) is a novel about the British rule in India.

- Graham Greene: *The Quiet American* (1955) is a novel set in Vietnam during the French colonial period.

- Romesh Gunesekera: *Heaven's Edge* (2003) is a novel set in Sri Lanka.

- E. M. Kaye: *Far Pavilions* (1978) is sometimes called India's *Gone with the Wind*.

- Rudyard Kipling: *The Man Who Would Be King* (1889) is set in India, and *Barrack-Room Ballads* (1891) is a collection of poems.

- Margaret Landon: *Anna and the King of Siam* (1903), about a governess who goes to Siam, was made into a Broadway musical and at least three films.

- Anchee Min: *Empress Orchid* (2004) is a novel about the last empress of China, who ruled for 46 years during the decline of the kingdom.

- Paul Scott: *The Raj Quartet* (1966–1975), an epic story of life in India during British rule, was made into Masterpiece Theater's series *The Jewel in the Crown*.

- Stanley Stewart: *In the Empire of Genghis Khan* (2002) is the author's experiences in a destination where few Westerners have ventured.

- Kent R. Weeks: *The Lost Tomb* (1998) is about an American Egyptologist who discovers the burial site of the sons of Ramesses II in 1995.

- Simon Winchester: He wrote *Krakatoa: The Day the World Exploded* (2003).

# Worksheet 14.1: Geography

| | |
|---|---|
| Name | Date |

**Directions:** Answer the questions in the space provided.

1. How would you describe the climate of India?

   _____

2. What are monsoons?

   _____

   _____

3. When would be the best time of year to visit Tokyo?

   _____

4. When is the best time of year to visit Beijing?

   _____

5. What is meant by the Ring of Fire?

   _____

   _____

6. You are heading west from North America toward the international date line on a Tuesday. After you pass over the date line, what day is it?

   _____

7. What countries are located on the long peninsula of Southeast Asia known as Indochina?

   _____

   _____

   _____

8. What mountain range forms the northern border of India?

   _____

9. What are China's two most important rivers?

   _____

10. Thailand's major river is the _____ .

11. How many time zones does China have?

   _____

12. Why does Bangladesh flood so often?

   _____

   _____

13. Which Asian country is in danger of disappearing if the ocean rises?

   _____

14. What four islands make up Japan?

   _____

   _____

15. What do the suffixes -*pur* and -*abad* mean?

   _____

16. Which South Asian country was never a European colony?

   _____

17. The world's highest peak, Mount Everest, is located in what Asian kingdom?

   _____

# Worksheet 14.2: Itinerary Planning

Name                                                                    Date

Outline a 2-week vacation for a couple to Thailand. Their interests include history, shopping, and outdoor activities.

# Worksheet 14.3: Answering Questions

_____
Name                                                                      Date

**Directions:** How would you respond to travelers who asked the following questions?

1. "What documentation do I need for my trip to Bhutan?"

2. "I won't be able to read the menus in Japan. What will I do?"

# Worksheet 14.4: Map Review: India and Southeast Asia

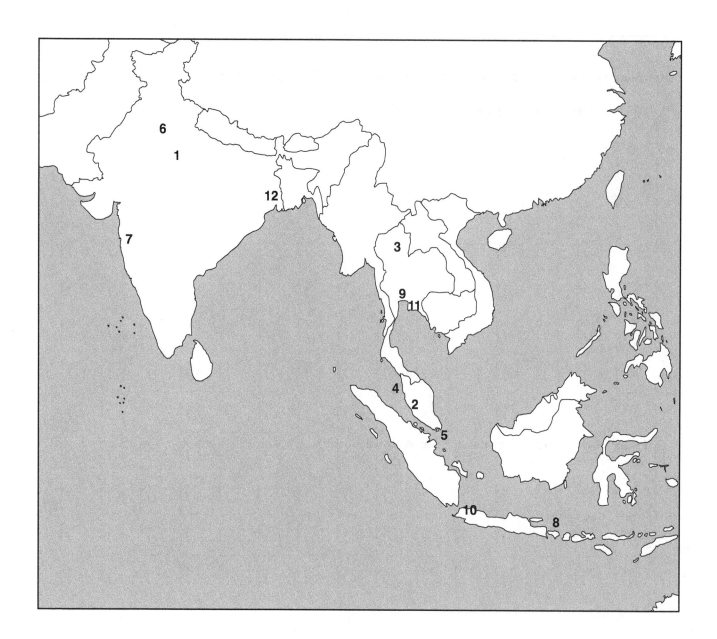

# Worksheet 14.4: Map Review: India and Southeast Asia

Name _____     Date

**Directions:** Match the destination below with the corresponding number on the map. Give the three-letter airport code of the destination or of the nearest airport.

**Map Number**                                        **Airport Code**

_____          Agra           _____

_____          Bali           _____

_____          Bangkok        _____

_____          Chiang Mai     _____

_____          Delhi          _____

_____          Jakarta        _____

_____          Kolkata        _____

_____          Kuala Lumpur   _____

_____          Mumbai         _____

_____          Penang         _____

_____          Phuket         _____

_____          Singapore      _____

**Bonus Question:** What famous mountain peak is located in Nepal?

_____

# Worksheet 14.4: Map Review: East Asia

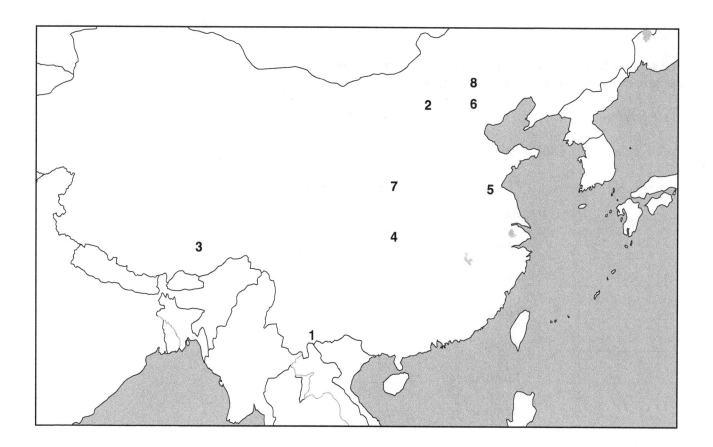

# Worksheet 14.5: Map Review: East Asia

Name _____ Date _____

**Directions:** Match the destination below with the corresponding number on the map. Give the three-letter code of the destination or of the nearest airport.

| Map Number | Destination | Airport Code |
|---|---|---|
| _____ | Forbidden City | _____ |
| _____ | Great Wall | _____ |
| _____ | Ming Tombs | _____ |
| _____ | Potala Palace | _____ |
| _____ | Silk Road | _____ |
| _____ | Stone Forest | _____ |
| _____ | Terracotta Warriors | _____ |
| _____ | Yangtze River Gorge | _____ |

**Bonus Questions**

1. What North American cities are on the same latitude as Beijing?

   _____

   _____

2. Which is farther south: Tokyo or Taiwan?

   _____

# Worksheet 14.6: Using Reference Materials

_____
Name                                                                Date

**Directions:** Using available resources, design a 2-week trip to China for a couple. Be sure to include plans for transportation to and around China, accommodations, and sightseeing. Indicate what resources you used.

Keep in mind:

- Market. Who are you designing the trip for?

- Budget. Is it practical?

- International dateline (IDL). Would you route the travelers east or west?

- Time. How long are the international flights?

- Documentation. What is needed for the areas you pick?

- Health. What does the CDC recommend?

- Safety. Are there any U.S. State Department advisories?

- Price. Can you come up with an approximate figure? Would it suit the budget of your couple?

# Worksheet 14.7: A Chapter Quiz

_____        _____
Name                                                                                    Date

**Directions:** Answer the questions in the space provided.

1. What is in the Taj Mahal? Where is the Taj Mahal located?

   _____

   _____

   _____

   _____

2. What is "Bollywood"?

   _____

   _____

   _____

   _____

3. Which Southeast Asian country is one of the world's richest? Why is it so rich?

   _____

   _____

   _____

   _____

4. What is done as a sign of respect before entering a temple, mosque, or private home?

   _____

5. **Directions:** Match each architectural work with its location.

   _____        Petronas Towers                    A. Java

   _____        Rock-carved temples                B. Kuala Lumpur

   _____        Snake Temple                       C. Ajanta

   _____        Borobudur                          D. Bangkok

   _____        Temple of the Emerald Buddha        E. Agra

   _____        Taj Mahal                          F. Penang

# Worksheet 14.8: Looking Back at East Asia: A Chapter Quiz

Name _____ Date _____

**Directions:** Circle the correct answer, or answer the questions in the space provided.

1. Indicate whether each statement is True or False.

   True     False     Mount Fuji is visible from Tokyo every day of the year.

   True     False     Honshu is the largest Japanese island.

   True     False     Tokyo is a sparsely populated city.

   True     False     The Ginza is an area of Tokyo known for its stores and nightclubs.

   True     False     The Shinkansen operate at speeds of up to 186 mph.

   True     False     In Japan, people drive on the right.

   True     False     China is the world's largest country.

   True     False     The best time to visit Beijing is spring or fall.

   True     False     After Beijing, Xi'an is China's most popular tourist destination.

   True     False     The 4-hour boat trip on the Li River near Guilin is an exceptional travel experience.

   True     False     In China, people drive on the left.

2. What destination is out of place in the itinerary Tokyo–Hakone–Nikko–Kyoto–Osaka–Taipei?

   _____

3. Which destination is out of place in the itinerary Beijing–Guangzhou–Guilin–Odense–Shanghai–Xi'an?

   _____

4. Which Chinese city is home to a maglev train?

   _____

5. How did Taiwan become independent of China?

   _____

   _____

   _____

   _____

6. Why isn't Tibet listed separately in Fast Facts in Appendix A of the *Exploring the World* textbook?

   _____

   _____

   _____

7.  What is the world's most commonly spoken language?

    _____

8.  Why has the completion date of China's Three Gorges Dam been important to tourism?

    _____

    _____

9.  What is the Forbidden City?

    _____

    _____

10. What transition took place within Hong Kong in 1997?

    _____

    _____

11. Why are North and South Korea separate countries?

    _____

    _____

    _____

    _____

12. Name two World Heritage attractions on the Indonesian island of Java.

    _____

    _____

# CHAPTER 15

# The Pacific

## ■ Resources

The tourist boards of both Australia and New Zealand promote their countries actively and provide many educational aids. The Pacific Asia Travel Association (PATA) provides information about Australia, New Zealand, and Oceania. Of the travel guides, the *Lonely Planet* series has its headquarters in Melbourne, Australia, so it is no wonder that writing about its own backyard is a specialty. The company publishes more than a dozen titles about the country down under.

As distant and diverse from one another as they are, fourteen islands of the South Pacific are represented by the South Pacific Tourism Organization (SPTO). The islands are Cook Islands, Fiji, Kiribati, Marshall Islands, Nauru, New Caledonia, Niue, Papua New Guinea, Samoa, Solomon Islands, Tahiti, Tonga, Tuvalu, and Vanuatu. You can link to information on each island or island group from SPTO's Web site.

### Australia
www.australia.com

Rail Australia
www.railaustralia.com.au

Visa Information
www.immi.gov.au

**Capital Territory**
www.canberratourism.com.au

**New South Wales**
www.tourism.nsw.gov.au

Bridgeclimb
www.bridgeclimb.com

Sydney Opera House
www.soh.nsw.gov.au

**Northern Territory**
www.insidetheoutback.com

Frontier Camel Farm
www.cameltours.com.au

Kakadu Park
www.biodiversity.environment.
gov.au/kakadu

**North Queensland**
www.tnq.org.au

**Queensland**
www.destinationqueensland.com

Brisbane Tourism
www.visitbrisbane.com.au

Gold Coast Tourism
www.goldcoasttourism.com.au

Great Barrier Reef
www.gbrmpa.gov.au

**South Australia**
www.southaustralia.com

**Tasmania**
www.tourism.tas.gov.au

Port Arthur
www.portarthur.org.au

**Victoria**
www.visitvictoria.com

**Western Australia**
www.westernaustralia.net

**New Zealand**
www.purenz.com

Automobile Association
www.nzaa.co.nz

New Zealand Rail
www.transzrail.co.nz

**South Pacific Islands**
www.southpacifictourism.org

# ■ UNESCO World Heritage Sites

For the Pacific, the UNESCO World Heritage List includes the following:

## Cultural Heritage

- Kakadu National Park, Australia

- Tasmanian wilderness, Australia

- Uluru-Kata Tjuta National Park, Australia

- Willandra Lakes region, Australia

## Natural Heritage

- Central and eastern rain forest reserves, Australia

- East Rennell, Solomon Islands

- Fiordland, Aoraki/Mount Cook and Westland National Parks, New Zealand

- Fraser Island, Australia

- Great Barrier Reef, Australia

- Greater Blue Mountains area, Australia

- Henderson Island, Pitcairn Islands

- Kakadu National Park, Australia

- Lord Howe Island group, Australia

- Naracoorte and Riversleigh mammalian fossil sites, Australia

- Queensland wet tropics, Australia

- Shark Bay, Australia

- Tasmanian wilderness, Australia

- Tongariro National Park, New Zealand

- Uluru-Kata Tjuta National Park, Australia

- Willandra Lakes Region, Australia

# Reading Suggestions: The Pacific

- Tony Horwitz: *Blue Latitudes* (2002) is part Cook biography, part travelogue.

- Robert Hughes: *The Fatal Shore*, (1986) a story of Australia, was made into a 9-hour series in 2000 for PBS titled *Beyond the Fatal Shore*.

- Keri Hulme: *The Bone People* is a novel about Maori characters; the author is part Maori.

- William Stuart Long: *The Australians* (1979–1987), which contains ten volumes, is an easy-to-read series of novels about the continent's settlement.

- Dame Ngaio Marsh: This New Zealander wrote detective stories.

- W. Somerset Maugham: *The Moon and the Sixpence* (1919) is based on the life of the artist Paul Gauguin.

- Colleen McCullough: *The Thorn Birds* (1977) is a story of an Outback station. McCullough is also author of *Morgan's Run* (2000), a saga about the first white settlers.

- Margaret Mead: *Coming of Age in Samoa* (1928) is a classic text in social anthropology, a study of adolescent girls in a noncompetitive culture.

- James A. Michener: He wrote *Tales of the South Pacific* (1947) and *Return to Paradise* (1951).

- George Plimpton: He edited *As Told at the Explorer's Club* (2003), fifty tales of adventure from Tahiti to Tibet and all compass points in between, from Explorer's Club members.

- Nevil Shute: *A Town Like Alice* (1950) and *On the Beach* (1957) are two novels set in Australia.

- Paul Theroux: *The Happy Isles of Oceania: Paddling the Pacific* (1992) is a nonfiction work on the problems of paradise.

# Worksheet 15.1: Geography

_____
Name                                                                      Date

**Directions:** Answer the questions in the space provided, or circle the correct answer.

1. What is Oceania?

   _____

   _____

2. Travelers who leave Los Angeles, California, on a nonstop flight on Friday, July 1, will arrive in Sydney, Australia, on
   A. Sunday, July 3.
   B. Saturday, July 2.
   C. Friday, July 1.
   D. Thursday, June 30.

3. Australia's hottest month, and the middle of its summer, is
   A. January.
   B. April.
   C. July.
   D. October.

4. In land area, Australia is almost the size of
   A. France.
   B. China.
   C. Peru.
   D. United States.

5. The Great Dividing Range runs down Australia's _____ coast.
   A. east
   B. west
   C. north
   D. south

6. What is a coral reef?

   _____

   _____

7. The Great Barrier Reef is off the Australian coast of
   A. New South Wales.
   B. Queensland.
   C. Victoria.
   D. South Australia.

8. Travelers seeking Australia's highest mountain should explore the Snowy Mountains in New South Wales and seek out
   A. Mount Kaputar.
   B. Mount Elliot.
   C. Mount Kosciuszko.
   D. Mount Cook.

9. Flowing mostly in South Australia, which river is the country's longest permanently flowing inland waterway?
   A. Avon
   B. Torrens
   C. Murray
   D. Swan

10. New Zealand is separated from Australia by the
    A. Arafura Sea.
    B. Milford Sound.
    C. Tasman Sea.
    D. Indian Ocean.

11. New Zealand's highest mountains are the
    A. Remarkables.
    B. Franz Josefs.
    C. Catlins.
    D. Southern Alps.

12. Bird-watchers seek New Zealand's elusive
    A. kakapo.
    B. emu.
    C. kiwi.
    D. bat.

13. Most North Americans traveling to New Zealand fly into the North Island city of
    A. Christchurch.
    B. Wellington.
    C. Dunedin.
    D. Auckland.

14. On New Zealand's South Island, the Southern Alps act as a barrier against the prevailing winds from the west, causing the west coast to have
    A. long, warm summers.
    B. a tropical climate.
    C. high rainfall.
    D. drought conditions.

15. What is Melanesia?

    _____

    _____

    _____

# Worksheet 15.1: Geography (continued)

_____

Name                                                              Date

16. What is an atoll?

_____

_____

17. Fiji's international gateway is _____ on the island of Viti Levu.
    A. Nadi
    B. Suva
    C. Nausori
    D. Lautoka

18. Papua New Guinea is on the _____ half of the island of New Guinea.
    A. northern
    B. southern
    C. eastern
    D. western

19. Travelers can cruise Papua New Guinea's _____ River on voyages of exploration to the island's interior.
    A. Fly
    B. Ramu
    C. Sepik
    D. Strickland

20. A broad expanse of sea with a large number of islands is called
    A. an atoll.
    B. an archipelago.
    C. a barrier reef.
    D. a group of cays.

21. What is Polynesia?

_____

_____

22. Heart-shaped _____ is the South Sea isle of the travel brochures.
    A. Tetiaroa
    B. Tutuila
    C. Moorea
    D. Aitutaki

23. _____ is an island near Japan with a large U.S. naval base.
    A. Tonga
    B. Fiji
    C. Guam
    D. Tahiti

# Worksheet 15.2: Itinerary Planning

Name                                                                    Date

The travelers have only a 2-week vacation and want to visit the Pacific region. They are very active and enjoy hiking and physically challenging activities. What would you suggest for them?

# Worksheet 15.3: Answering Questions

_____
Name                                                        Date

**Directions:** How would you respond to travelers who asked the following questions?

1. "Isn't a trip to Australia very expensive?"

2. "Isn't New Zealand just a lot of scenery and outdoor activities?"

3. "Can I see the places in New Zealand where the _Lord of the Rings_ trilogy was filmed?"

# Worksheet 15.4: Map Review

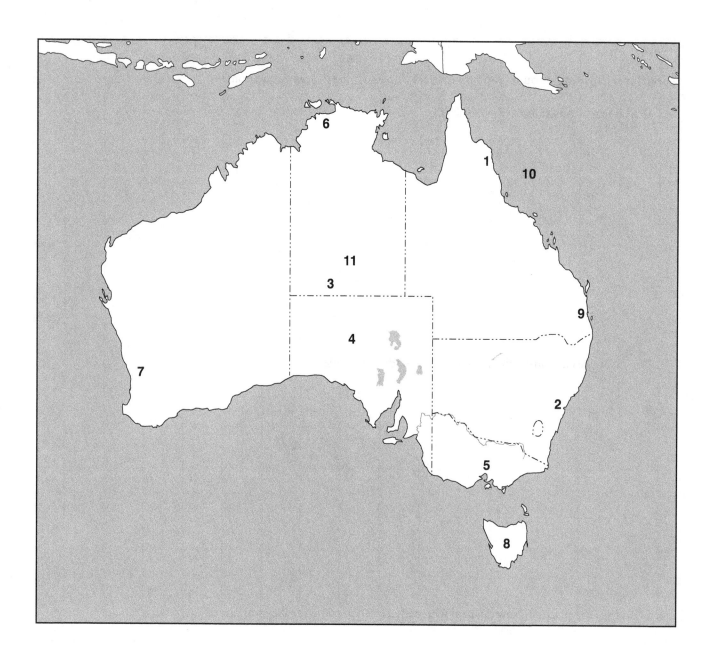

# Worksheet 15.4: Map Review

_____

Name                                                                    Date

**Directions:** Match the destination listed with its corresponding letter on the map. Give the three-letter airport code of the destination or of the nearest airport.

**Map Number**                                    **Airport Code**

_____        Alice Springs          _____

_____        Brisbane               _____

_____        Cairns                 _____

_____        Coober Pedy            _____

_____        Darwin                 _____

_____        Great Barrier Reef     _____

_____        Hobart                 _____

_____        Melbourne              _____

_____        Perth                  _____

_____        Sydney                 _____

_____        Uluru (Ayers Rock)     _____

**Bonus Question:** Name the highest mountain in Papua New Guinea.

_____

# Worksheet 15.5: Using Reference Materials

Name _____ Date _____

**Directions:** Using available resources, answer the questions in the space provided. Indicate in your answer what resource you used.

1. From your city, how would you route travelers who want to fly to Australia and New Zealand?

2. What documentation do they need to visit Australia? New Zealand?

3. What type of hotel accommodations are available in Alice Springs?

4. Are there any special events in either Australia or New Zealand that you think the travelers would enjoy?

# Worksheet 15.6: Looking Back: A Chapter Quiz

Name                                                                          Date

**Directions:** Circle the correct answer, or write the answer in the space provided.

1. Ayers Rock is closest to the Outback town of
   A. Coober Pedy.
   B. Alice Springs.
   C. Broken Hill.
   D. Broome.

2. The Indian Pacific Railway offers a train ride across the Nullabor Plain between
   A. Cairns and Darwin.
   B. Brisbane and Alice Springs.
   C. Canberra and Adelaide.
   D. Perth and Sydney.

3. Australia's famous opera house designed by Danish architect Joern Utzum is found in
   A. Canberra.
   B. Brisbane.
   C. Melbourne.
   D. Sydney.

4. The gateway for 99 percent of North American travelers to the Great Barrier Reef is the city of
   A. Cairns.
   B. Port Douglas.
   C. Brisbane.
   D. Townsville.

5. New Zealand's largest city is
   A. Auckland.
   B. Christchurch.
   C. Wellington.
   D. Invercargill.

6. The world-renowned Milford Track is found in _____ National Park.
   A. Fiordland
   B. Egmont
   C. Tongariro
   D. Mount Cook

7. New Zealand's capital city is
   A. Auckland.
   B. Christchurch.
   C. Hamilton.
   D. Wellington.

8. _____ is the starting point for the 5-day hike to Milford Sound.
   A. Invercargill
   B. Queenstown
   C. Twizel
   D. Te Anau

9. The Maori equivalent of a luau is called a
   A. *pakha*.
   B. *hangi*.
   C. *meke*.
   D. *kumara*.

10. Match the place-names with the descriptions that follow.

   Fiji          Guam          Tonga          Tahiti          Papua New Guinea

   _____  A. It is composed of about 170 islands south of the
                                        equator and just west of the international date line and
                                        is the only remaining kingdom in the Pacific.

   _____  B. It is called the "Crossroads of the South Pacific," Viti
                                        Levu and Vanua Levu are its two largest islands.

   _____  C. Sing-sing Festivals and primitive art are just two of
                                        the attractions of this country.

   _____  D. This is an island near Japan with a large U.S. naval
                                        base.

   _____  E. This is one of the Society Islands of French Polynesia
                                        and is known for its capital, the city of Papeete.

# An Exclusive Career Opportunity

Students who complete a course of study using *Exploring the World* have a unique opportunity for career advancement. It's the Geography for Travel Professionals Test Certificate. When students pass the Geography for Travel Professionals Test, they receive the Geography for Travel Professionals Test Certificate. Here's how the process works.

## Step One

Students complete a course that is based chiefly on *Exploring the World*.

## Step Two

Students who want to participate in the testing program fill out the Test Request form at www.thetravelinstitute.com/testing and pay an administrative fee of $25. The paper test has an additional charge of $25.

The test consists of 100 multiple-choice questions, and students have up to two hours to complete it.

The Institute awards a passing grade to students who earn a score of 70 percent or better.

## Step Three

Students who earn a passing grade receive the Geography for Travel Professionals Test Certificate from the instructor. The certificate gives beginning travel professionals a competitive edge in the marketplace.

## Sample Test Questions

Here are a few examples of questions on the Geography for Travel Professionals Test.

1. If it is 5:00 PM in Los Angeles, California (GMT –8), what time is it in Bermuda (GMT – 4)?
   A. 2:00 PM
   B. 9:00 PM
   C. 2:00 AM
   D. 1:00 PM

2. The south coast of the Iberian Peninsula has dry, warm summers and winters that are
   A. long and cold.
   B. snowy.
   C. hot and sunny.
   D. mild and rainy.

3. Which destination is out of place in this list of New England attractions?
   A. Mad River Valley
   B. Freedom Trail
   C. Liberty Bell
   D. The Breakers

4. From the popular resort of Cancún in Mexico, tourists on day excursions can visit the Mayan ruins of
   A. Tulúm.
   B. Teotihuacán.
   C. Altun Ha.
   D. Tikal.

5. Accommodations in Spain include the government-run chain of three- to five-star hotels located in castles, former convents, medieval fortresses, and modern properties known as
   A. *pousadas.*
   B. paradores.
   C. pensions.
   D. *albergos.*